CREATIVE DIRECTIONS

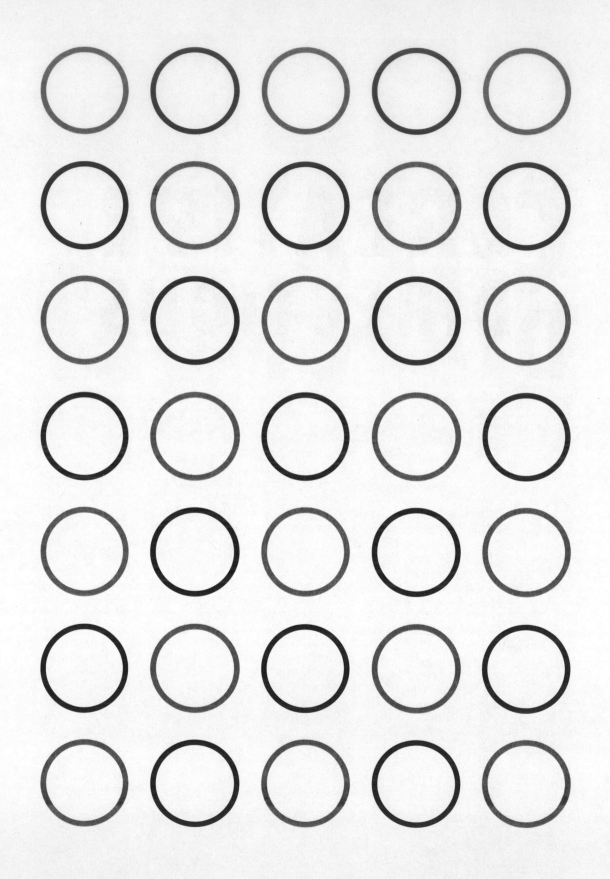

JASON SPERLING

CREATIVE DIRECTIONS

MASTERING THE MOVE FROM TALENT TO LEADER

HarperCollins
LEADERSHIP

An Imprint of HarperCollins

Published by HarperCollins Leadership, an imprint of HarperCollins Focus LLC.

Any internet addresses, phone numbers, or company or product information printed in this book are offered as a resource and are not intended in any way to be or to imply an endorsement by HarperCollins Leadership, nor does HarperCollins Leadership vouch for the existence, content, or services of these sites, phone numbers, companies, or products beyond the life of this book.

Book design by Aubrey Khan, Neuwirth & Associates.

ISBN 978-1-4002-2290-2 (eBook)
ISBN 978-1-4002-2289-6 (HC)

Library of Congress Control Number: 2021934462

Printed in the United States of America
21 22 23 LSC 10 9 8 7 6 5 4 3 2 1

CONTENTS

SECTION 1

MANAGING PEOPLE

CONTRIBUTORS

MIKE ALDERSON—Cofounder and Chief Creative Officer, Man vs. Machine

DAVID ANGELO—President, David & Goliath

MARQUIS AVERY—Creative Director, TikTok

SARAH MAY BATES—VP, Creative Director, RPA; Director, Podcaster, Founder, *Yay With Me*

JENI BRITTON BAUER—Founder, Chief Creative Officer, Jeni's Ice Cream

SAM BERGEN—Chief Creative Officer, Beats by Dre

EZ BLAINE—Executive Creative Director, ChowNow

JONATHAN CAVENDISH—Producer, *Bridget Jones's Diary, Elizabeth:* *The Golden Age*; *Mowgli: Legend of the Jungle*; Founder, The Imaginarium Studios

MARCELLA COAD—Creative Director, Amazon

RICK COLBY—former President, Executive Creative Director, Colby & Partners Dentsu

SUSAN CREDLE—Global Chief Creative Officer, FCB Global

ALICIA DOTTER—360 Senior Creative Director, Amazon

MATT DRENIK—Creative Director, SOUTH Music; Recording Artist, Sony Music Entertainment

AVA DUVERNAY—Executive Producer, *Queen Sugar*; Director, *When They See Us, Selma, A Wrinkle in Time*

JEFF GILES—Senior Editor, *Vanity Fair*

JEFF GOODBY—
President, Goodby Silverstein Advertising

DAVIS GUGGENHEIM—
Producer and Director, *Deadwood,*
Melrose Place, An Inconvenient Truth,
Waiting for Superman, It Might Get Loud

SUSAN HOFFMAN—
Chairman, Wieden & Kennedy

JON IKEDA—VP, Acura Brand Officer
and former Lead Designer, Acura

LANCE JENSEN—
Executive Vice President,
Chief Creative Officer, Hill Holliday

MARGARET JOHNSON—CCO and
Partner, Goodby Silverstein & Partners

MARGARET KEENE—
Executive Creative Director, Mullen LA

BRIAN KELLEY—
Co-Executive Producer, *The Simpsons*

ROB LADUCA—Executive Producer,
Mickey Mouse Clubhouse; Effects Animator,
Star Wars: Episode VI—Return of the Jedi

TIM LEAKE—
Chief Marketing Officer, RPA

MICHAEL LEJEUNE—
Creative Director, Metro Los Angeles

EMILY MCDOWELL—Founder, Creative
Director, Emily McDowell & Friends; Author,
There Is No Good Card for This

SCOTT MARDER—
Executive Producer, *Rick and Morty,*
The Mick, Always Sunny in Philadelphia

BRIAN MILLER—
Creative Director, The Walt Disney
Company/Global Marketing

SEEMA MILLER—
Cofounder, President, Wolfgang

DUNCAN MILNER—
Former Global Creative President,
Media Arts Lab, MAL For Good

KRISTEN GROVE MØLLER—
Creative Director, 72andSunny

CHUCK MONN—
Group Creative Director, Media Arts Lab

RAVI NAIDOO—Founder,
Interactive Africa, Design Indaba

SURESH NAIR—Global Chief
Strategy Officer, Grey Worldwide

TIM NUDD—
Editor-in-Chief, *Muse by Clio*

SAM OLIVER—
Group Creative Director, Apple

CHRIS ORD—Executive Producer,
Covert Affairs, Containment, The Enemy
Within, The Brave, Girls on the Bus

DAVID OYELOWO—
Actor, *Selma;* Producer, *Come Away;*
Director, *The Water Man*

TED PRICE—
President and Founder, Insomniac Games

RON RADZINER—
President, Design Partner,
Marmol Radziner Architects

JAMIE REILLY—
Global Creative Director, Vans

JOE RUSSO—Executive Producer,
Community; Director, *Avengers: Endgame;*
Founder, Bullitt Productions

ROB SCHWARTZ—
Chief Executive Officer,
TBWA\Chiat\Day, New York

RACHEL SHUKERT—
Co-Executive Producer, *GLOW;*
Executive Producer, *The Baby-Sitters Club*

GUTO TERNI—
Partner, Director, ROOF Animation Studio

SCOTT TRATTNER—
VP, Creative, Airbnb, former VP,
Executive Creative Director, Facebook

VALERIE VAN GALDER—
CEO, Depressed Cake Shop; former
President of Marketing, Sony Pictures

ANGUS WALL—
Producer, *13th ;* Editor, *The Girl with the
Dragon Tattoo, The Social Network;* Founder,
Rock Paper Scissors Editorial, A52, Elastic

MATTHEW WARD—Creative Director,
Cinematic Director, Bungie Games

SHANNON WASHINGTON—
Group Executive Creative Director, R/GA

ALISON WATSON—
Partner, Founder, Legacy House;
Owner-President, Four Sisters Productions;
former Director, Grind Studios

TARAS WAYNER—
Chief Creative Officer, Saatchi & Saatchi

MARC WEINSTOCK—
President, Worldwide Marketing &
Distribution, Paramount Pictures

BARRY WEISS—Founder, President,
RECORDS; former CEO, RCA/Jive Records;
former Chairman, UMG East Coast Labels

XANTHE WELLS—
Senior Director, Global Executive Creative
Director, Devices & Services, Google

BILL WESTBROOK—
Chief Executive Officer, No Fences
Consulting; former President, Executive
Creative Director, Fallon Worldwide

INTRODUCTION

LET ME BE CLEAR: I never wanted to be a manager. I had no great aspirations to wear suit jackets to meet with clients about launch schedules, budget allocations, or market strategies. I wasn't hoping to give performance reviews to anxious employees, or determine who gets an office with a window and who gets a cubicle near the bathrooms.

I just wanted to *make* things. If I was fortunate, some really great things.

But after several years and stints at various ad agencies, the dreaded inevitable happened: I was promoted. My success earned me the title of Creative Director, then Group Creative Director, and eventually Chief of Creative Development. With each successive promotion came a host of new responsibilities, most of which . . . weren't very creative at all. I went from spending the bulk of my days writing and producing campaigns for Apple to managing people, project oversight, interfacing with clients, talent recruitment, budget planning, employee reviews, pitching new business, and—*gasp*—even reviewing time sheets! Suddenly, sometimes quite unexpectedly, and with little transition time and even less training, we go from unstructured, imaginative thinkers to (hopefully) responsible leaders. We go from a world of making things to managing things. The potential to suck is incredibly high. Art school had trained me to strategize and conceive marketing campaigns (and, on occasion, how to draw a nude man's figure in charcoal, which comes in surprisingly handy), but it didn't teach me anything about this.

The thing is, my story is not all that different from a lot of others. Many of us who've found success in the commercial creative world have the lucrative but unenviable position of moving up and out of those creative roles that we were so good at. Our good fortune becomes a springboard into becoming a creative leader, and—ironically—moves us further away from the creative thinking that got us there in the first place. Put simply: the reward for being good at our job is to do a largely different job that we don't have the natural skill set or qualifications for, and might not be good at. Because we were great at making things, people suddenly think we can be great at leading things. Which, when you think about it, is a recipe for total disaster.

The irony isn't lost on Emily McDowell, founder and Creative Director at Emily Mc-Dowell & Friends. "Being a creative leader is the only job where, in order to get the job, you have to be really good at this other job, which ultimately doesn't have very much to do with the new job you end up doing."

Creative people don't necessarily possess the traits (or well-ironed dress shirts, for that matter) of what we consider typical leaders. According to *Forbes* that includes things like being an effective communicator and motivator, being a self-manager and team builder, being able to set clear goals for people, and being an agile strategist. Creative people are a different breed and often deviate from the norm. For one, we're unstructured thinkers, which makes us really great at coming up with surprising, unorthodox ideas and solutions, but not so great for managing projects, delegating work, adhering to timelines, or supervising people. Creative people are typically governed by passion, emotion, and most importantly, our imaginations, with instinct often eclipsing logic. What makes us "prone to epiphanies" often runs counter to what makes people great managers. In fact, it's a completely separate set of skills. As Rachel Shukert, writer and co-executive producer of the Netflix show *GLOW*, puts it, "Writers often spend years of their working life working alone, and become writers because they don't have the best people skills and don't feel comfortable working in groups. Suddenly [when they join a writer's room] they're being asked to externalize what is inherently an internal process."

While creative people have an arsenal of unique skills that set them apart, we're typically not known for things like pragmatism, order, or reason. (Little things. Not even that important, really.) In an interview with *The Neuroscience of Creativity* author Anna Abraham, she says, "The creative mode involves turning away from the path of least resistance and venturing into the briars so to speak in an effort to forge a new path through the gray zone of the unexpected, the vague, the misleading, or the unknown." When talking about the process, Wieden + Kennedy founder Dan Wieden says, "Chaos is the only friend who really helps you be creative." What makes a creative person so good at writing music, penning novels, directing and editing movies (or, in my case, churning out a semi-decent fifteen-second ad) is an ability to free-form associate and amalgamate disparate thoughts, feelings, memories, stories, and sensations that don't necessarily make it through other people's mental filters. Consider the classic "Think Different" ad campaign from Apple that showcased many famous creative thinkers. It started with the words, "Here's to the crazy ones. The misfits. The rebels. The troublemakers. The ones who see things differently." That's creative people. We think different (or differently if you're into proper English).

Another big obstacle for creative people transitioning into leadership is the notion of shared success, something that creative leaders are required to embrace but which doesn't necessarily come easily or naturally. Making things has been something that we do for ourselves (and to keep our jobs in extremely competitive creative industries). At its most modest, it comes from a need for self-expression and personal fulfillment. But there's also typically a broader connection to ego, identity, and survival. When we make something great, it makes us feel great. When it gets attention, we feel talented. When we become a creative leader, we're required to put our own egos and insecurities aside, as well as the instinctual drive to "create for ourselves," in order to be mindful of our departments and companies. Now, that drive to outdo our peers has to be re-channeled into enabling the entire group to succeed and advocating on behalf of others (some of whom might even have been your peers and people you competed against). In our new leadership positions, we have to watch other people get celebrated, revered, and envied. That can be a lot for a creative person to take.

Environment also plays a big role in creativity, which is why so many creatively focused companies design inspiring spaces for their makers and give them the freedom to come and go as they please. TV writers sit in writer's rooms for hours yelling jokes over one another. Advertising creative teams will sit behind closed doors bouncing ideas until they hate each other, or work outside the office in coffeehouses and cafés where their minds are free to wander. The switch to a leadership role, and from maker to manager, necessarily impacts those freedoms. We're asked to be more present in the office and potentially—*gasp*—become involved in corporate culture. That free-spirited, rambunctious mentality that was once central to who we are and how we think makes the tethering to an office that much more dispiriting. It's as if we're trading out a lifetime of sketchpads for lined notebooks.

The point of all of this is to say that much of what makes the transition so difficult is inherent to those of us making the transition. Our very nature and creative instincts are great for developing work, but not necessarily for managing it. We're used to roles that allow us room for play, not professionalism. Yet we're consistently thrust into leadership positions where we're asked to do things that don't mesh with our skill sets. As Jeff Goodby, Co-Chairman and Partner at ad agency Goodby Silverstein & Partners, puts it: "To become a creative director, you have to overcome years of competing with other creative people for assignments and awards, and suddenly embrace a fresh kind of support for everyone around you. You have to find a way to tell your people the truth, forgive their missteps, and help them get up off the floor after rejection—including, and especially, rejection by you."

As for training, many organizations still don't have a formal program in place to help foster managerial skills, and certainly not one that's tailored specifically to the creative person. It's still a trial-by-fire process, where you get thrown blindly into the role to see whether you quite miraculously show a natural perspicacity for leadership, or if you're doomed to replicate the mistakes of prior leaders. As one person said at a leadership conference panel I attended, "You get better management training at a fast-food restaurant than you do in most creative departments."

And, even if you were an incredible, award-winning creative person in your field with a long resume of critical successes, there's no assurance that the move to leader will lead to similar acclaim. Experience will teach you a lot, but not everything. In fact, plenty of people make the leap and never develop into effective managers, either because they don't evolve their way of thinking, don't have the acumen for a managerial role, or prioritize their ego and don't remove themselves from the daily process of making things. And far too often, talented and creative people get burned by leaders who aren't fit or prepared for the job. "Some of the people who come up with the best ideas are totally unfit to be put in positions of any responsibility, let alone put in charge of someone else's career," says Jamie Reilly, Global Creative Director at Vans.

Adds Jeni Britton Bauer, founder and Creative Director of Jeni's Splendid Ice Creams, "What got you here won't get you there." I saw plenty of this when I was starting out. My first creative director would routinely dress down employees without any concern for undermining people's authority or embarrassing them in front of their peers. If you complained, he'd say things like, "Don't be a bitch, Sperling." When the volatility and fraternity-house antics became too much for me to handle there, I fled to a small agency run by a creative director who was disengaged, passive-aggressive, and played favorites among our small creative group. He'd also rewrite your copy right after you went home for the day, without notice and without any feedback (not that changing my words for an iceberg lettuce print ad was going to ruin my shot at fame and fortune). And there were plenty more bad role models to come after that.

But this isn't just about being an effective leader. Beyond the short-term dopamine hit that comes with the raise and fancy new title, will you actually *enjoy* the role? According to Sam Bergen, Chief Creative Officer at Beats by Dre, "The difficulty is compounded, and things are far more complex the more senior you grow. You have to remain authentic to yourself or else you're going to be unhappy." Many people make the move because they feel it is the natural next step in their career, or the key to making more money, or can't bear to see other people at their level become their boss. But they don't consider whether they will be as happy or fulfilled stepping aside to focus on those managerial tasks. And for the companies who dole out the promotions, they have to consider the drawbacks of moving essential creative talent into supervisory roles. But that's another issue for another book.

This phenomenon isn't specific to those of us who work inside companies; some talented creative people go on to start their own businesses. That's a lot more freedom to create whatever you want to create—but now you have to run a company, which means hiring, firing, overseeing, keeping clients happy, balancing budgets, and choosing the artwork that hangs inside the lobby. (Okay, that last one's probably pretty fun.)

Sure, a ridiculous number of books have been written on how to be a great manager and leader. But very little has been written specifically for the creative person who is transitioning into a leadership position. Given that this role isn't necessarily a natural fit, there's an even greater need for a resource that is specific to the creative audience, both in terms of content and presentation. This book is a collection of wisdom spanning the many unique aspects and challenges of transitioning to creative leadership positions. It offers advice in five key areas:

1. Managing employees
2. Managing clients and higher-ups
3. Being a leader
4. The work
5. Career

I hope that you find this book a valuable resource, no matter what field or stage of career you're in. It's something I wish I had when I made the transition to being a leader, a sentiment that was echoed by almost every contributor whose advice is in these pages. Susan Hoffman, chairman of Wieden & Kennedy, told me she spent years screwing up. And David Angelo, founder and chairman of David & Goliath, admits it took him at least ten years to learn and earn that title after being promoted. As for myself, I felt rudderless and blind at the start (deepest apologies to all those poor writers, art directors, and account folks who had to suffer through my early on-the-job training). Instinctually, I knew to champion the work of my teams, to share in the successes and to employ many of the philosophical notions that are now bundled together as "servant leadership," but I certainly struggled with aspects of my new role. Too often, in an effort to prove to myself and to my team that I was capable of being a creative leader, I unnecessarily inserted myself into the creative process and diluted the pool of ideas with my own, which—shocking to no one—I thought were kind of amazing. I didn't give my team opportunities to pitch their work to bosses for fear that they wouldn't sell them with the necessary conviction. And I often picked fights with leads in other departments who weren't aligned with my vision (my *reply all* email battles to one lead in particular were the stuff of legend at my former advertising agency, RPA). Even though I genuinely wanted the people working for me to grow and flourish, and wanted to instill pride and help strengthen our agency's reputation, I was sowing seeds of discontent and causing resentment among my peers. It didn't matter that my intentions were mostly noble. As one early review I received from a superior at RPA put it, "The work your team did this year was great, but unfortunately the work isn't everything."

This book is not meant to be a step-by-step manual but rather a collection of insights that can help inform you along your own leadership journey. The aim is that it erases (being hopeful) or reduces (being realistic) the learning curve that I and so many others have had to deal with on the way to taking on leadership roles. And it's intended to help those of us who are already in leadership roles improve on what we do, and correct bad habits before we negatively impact the careers of others or submarine our own careers. This is not intended to be your typical tome of managerial wisdom, dry as an almanac and dense as a Tolstoy novel. It's not meant for the Wharton Business School crowd. Far from it. This book is for a special type of manager: the unorthodox outlier that powers corporate creativity up to its highest levels. Thus, it's a different type of management book. It's visual, conversational, quotable, concise, and full of valuable insights.

While my experience comes from over two decades as a leader in the advertising field, the guidance in the pages that follow is intended to serve a much broader creative community. An expanse of commercial arts careers, which, besides being their own lucrative industries, include positions in every Fortune 500 company. The book contains contributions from respected leaders that span a variety of creative careers—from design, animation, television and film production and post-production, technology, culinary, architecture, music, and marketing. Included within are perspectives from chief creative officers, creative directors, executive producers, senior editors, senior animators, founders, and presidents from companies like Google, Amazon, Apple, Facebook, Beats by Dre, Vans, TikTok, and Paramount Pictures. It includes luminaries like Ava DuVernay (*When They See Us*), Davis Guggenheim (*Waiting for Superman*), and Joe Russo (*Avengers: Endgame*); two-time Academy Award–winning editor Angus Wall (*The Social Network*); executive producers Brian Kelley (*The Simpsons*), Scott Marder (*Rick & Morty*), and Rachel Shukert (*GLOW*); and Jeff Giles, *Vanity Fair* editor. Every contributor was once a vital creative talent and is now a leader within their respective organization and field (and many still actively practice their craft, as well). Together, they lend their observations, stories, and wisdom, making this an important book for any creative leader or leader-to-be. There are many creative directions here to choose from as you decide on what fits you best.

Let's get to the good stuff.

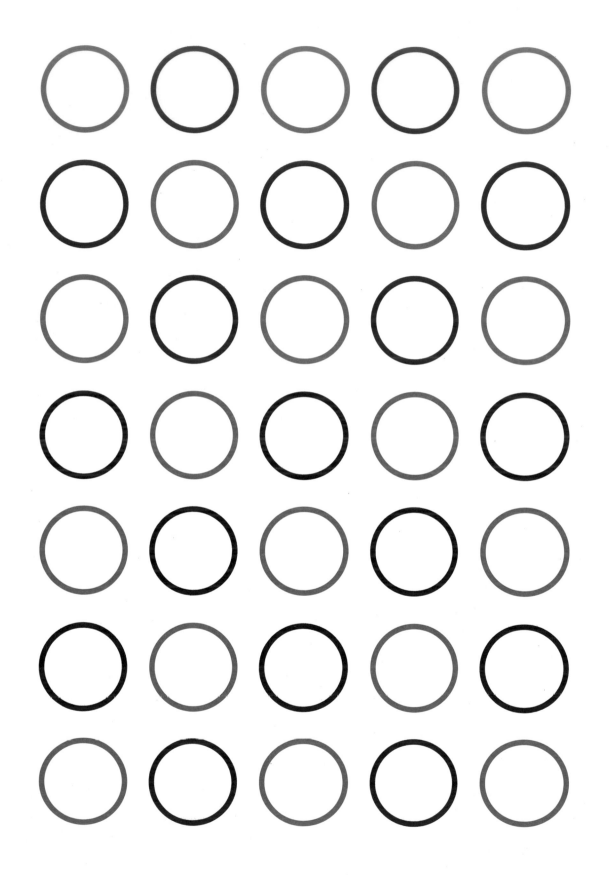

MANAGING
PEOPLE

SECTION 1
MANAGING PEOPLE

Up until now you have been a maker, an artist, or a creator. The only thing you were in charge of were ideas, and the biggest problems you faced were coming up with new good ones. And now, as a reward for your success, you have been put in charge of *people*, and people . . . are vastly more complicated. They require oversight, direction, feedback, and support. They have varying degrees of ambition and talent. They have differing perspectives about management, your involvement in their work, and their level of investment in your company. And no one is quite the same.

Your role and work relationships have evolved and are more complex than ever before. But it's not easy for everyone to transition to the new role. When I was first promoted to manager, I thought that the people on my team would automatically take to my new role and offer me their full support and enthusiasm. That they would all work productively and independently and leave me to focus on my job for the most part. It was much more complicated than that. Whatever feelings of support my team felt quickly—and rightfully—shifted to, "How will this affect my day-to-day happiness, growth potential, and job effectiveness?" I had to deal with the frustration of former peers who were now working underneath me, the wariness of senior team members, and the tenuous relationships of an extremely talented yet tough-to-please creative department. I definitely had my hands full.

As Jeni Britton Bauer, founder and Creative Director of Jeni's Splendid Ice Creams, puts it, "Those people you were in the trenches with now look to you for direction and so your attitude has to change."

Says Emily McDowell, founder and Creative Director at Emily McDowell & Friends, "I really didn't know what I was doing. I was a boss and creating this hierarchy, but still wanted to be everyone's friend. I was trying to get my MBA from searching Google every night."

Adds Marc Weinstock, President of Worldwide Marketing and Distribution at Paramount Pictures, "You don't just go to lunch with the staff anymore. Now it's considered a lunchtime work meeting, and they expect you to pick up the tab. You miss the old times."

The jump to a managerial role poses a whole new set of challenges for you, and creates a new set of pressures that are guaranteed to make you double your supply of antacids and grind your nightguard into a fine powder. How do you balance getting what you need while giving your employees what *they* need to be happy, fulfilled, and successful . . . potentially while working remotely full-time? How does "manager you" relate to the people making things—some of whom might very well have been friends of yours from your years in the trenches? And how do you maintain a supportive yet creative work environment where people are willing to bring the kind of brave breakthrough ideas that get attention and acclaim?

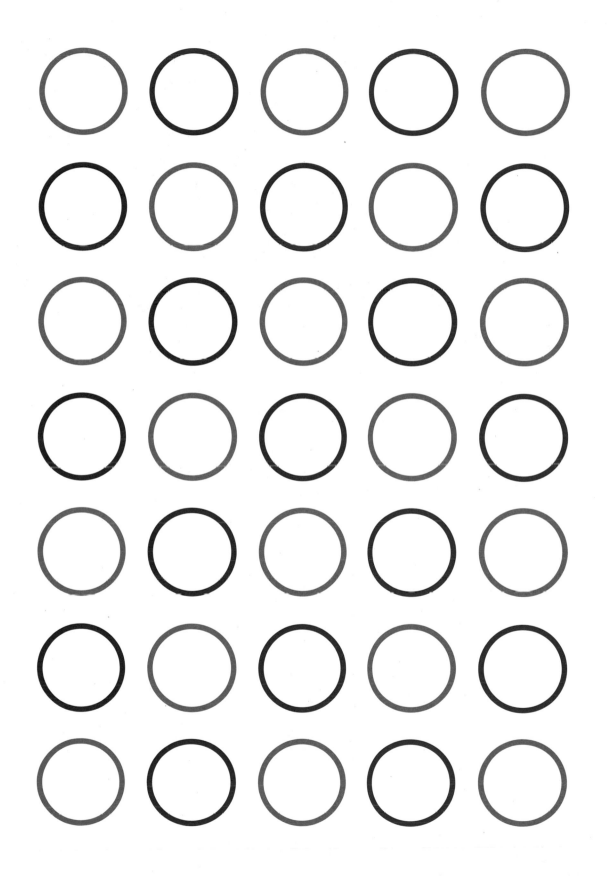

TRADE THE

SPOTLIGHT

for

FLASHLIGHTS

TRADE THE
SPOTLIGHT
FOR FLASHLIGHTS.

As a creative person, the goal was as simple as they come: make yourself the focus of attention. Once your work is noticed, you (the work's obviously talented and irreplaceable maker) will be noticed, too. Given that our career survival depends on the things we make and how well they're received by clients, the public, and judgy peers, there's nothing wrong with that approach. However, when you become a leader, all that needs to change.

As the leader of a team, it's important to recognize that it's not just about you anymore. Avoid the "me, me, me minefield," which can hold you back at this point in your career. There are people depending on you to help them figure out how to arrive at great ideas, improve their craft, and build a body of work that will earn them a share of the spotlight. They want to feel supported by you and heard, to receive mentorship opportunities, and know that their individual well-being is being taken into consideration.

Some leaders are ready to shed their "maker" skin, metamorphose into selfless guides, and open their large coffers of knowledge. But remember—your success and your team's success are closely intertwined. For those insecure leaders who still need that ego gratification and need to be the focal point of attention, there can be unintended long- and short-term consequences. It can erode loyalty and trust within the groups you manage, stifle growth within your company, and lead to job dissatisfaction and—worst of all—a loss of creative talent.

JOE RUSSO

Executive Producer, *Community*; Director,
Avengers: Endgame; Founder, Bullitt Productions

ANTHONY [RUSSO] AND I were fortunate to have mentors along the way that have helped us and offered real-world advice. After the premiere of our first film in Slamdance, *PIECES*, Steven Soderbergh became our first champion, guiding us through the next several years of our careers. Having a mentor does not mean that everything moves along quickly, but it does help give you a foundation to stand on. It's always up to us to find and communicate our vision, but it helps enormously to have that support in our corner.

JAMIE REILLY

VP Global Creative, Vans

YOU ARE NOW in charge of other people's careers. That means listening to a lot of ideas that are in different stages: some bad, some good, some great. Your job is to kill the bad ones (and explain why), make the good ones great, and leave the great ones alone. And, no matter how much work you did to make a good idea great, it still came from your team, so *they* get the credit. This is a hard one for some people. You know how at the end of a musical, when everyone is taking their bows and the spotlight is on the star and the applause is at its loudest, the star gestures down to the orchestra pit and the lights drop and you see the people who have been invisibly powering the entire thing the whole time? That seems like the right culture to me.

As the creative director, even when you're the face of your department or your company, you should always point out, "I'm simply the waiter. The delicious things you have been eating were made possible by a whole staff of people who put their sweat and souls into making this exquisite thing. I just deliver it to the table." (I know I am mixing metaphors. Get over it. There are probably more coming.)

And it's not just your team, by the way. Motherf-ers work hard as hell and never get thanked: producers, strategists, developers, storyboard artists, the list is long. *You* have the sexy job here, so give props to all the people who make you look good, and don't ever forget the importance of the backup band. Trust me, you're not going to sound more like Lou Costello than Freddie Mercury if they isolate your vocals.

ANGUS WALL

Producer, *13th*; Editor, *Girl with the Dragon Tattoo*,
The Social Network; Founder, Rock Paper Scissors
Editorial, A52, Elastic

MAYBE IT'S SYMPTOMATIC of getting older, but the reason you do what you do changes over your lifetime. It may start with, "Can I hold down a job? Can I make something that has value for someone? Can I get really good at something?" But ultimately you get to a point where you've achieved certain things. You don't need to feed your own ego anymore and you're no longer trying to succeed in order to survive. Now you can make it easier for other people to do those things, and the question becomes, "How do I make an ecosystem that helps people explore the outer edges of what they're capable of doing?"

In a weird way, success for creative people is survival. When you're younger, you're just trying to survive long enough to where you don't feel the pressure to make something every single day. Now the challenge is to continue to create systems and infrastructure that helps other people be successful, which has its own peculiar joy.

Ultimately you want everyone to learn to make their own decisions. You want people to realize not how you would do something but how they would do it. You want to co-pilot, but you want them to drive and to navigate. There are times when you lead and times when you listen. Sometimes input, sometimes output, sometimes it's all shared. The role is never standardized.

SUSAN CREDLE

Global Chief Creative Officer, FCB Global

ONE OF THE things I see with people moving into leadership positions early on is they have this desire to prove that they deserve that position. They steal all the quotes in news articles written about their work, they take all the credit, they want to be on every award show jury. I think it all comes from a place of proving "I deserve this job."

The leaders that can be generous are the true leaders of today. But it's hard to share and give away credit on work, to step out of the spotlight and put other people in it, to give people the benefit of the doubt. We have a lot of ego and insecurity, and we naturally default to taking care of ourselves and making sure people know how great we still are.

For me, the managing or leading of great creatives is more fulfilling than when I was on the front line doing the work myself.

SHANNON WASHINGTON

Group Executive Creative Director, R/GA

I'M NOT YODA. I'm not perfect. I'm not at my pinnacle just yet. But if I can help you improve on something, and if you can say that after working under my guidance you were able to develop something great or somehow improve . . . I believe that I've done my job the right way. It's not just creating great work but creating great creatives. It's about helping career paths.

BARRY WEISS

Founder, President, RECORDS; former CEO, RCA/Jive Records; former Chairman, UMG East Coast Labels

I THINK IT'S a competitive advantage of mine that I don't have an ego. I think you should have pride and confidence, but not an ego. As one of my mentors, Clive Calder, said to me, "That thing is a tailwind against you."

BRIAN MILLER

Creative Director, The Walt Disney Company/ Global Marketing

AS YOUNG CREATIVE people in advertising, we've all had that associate creative director or creative director who concepted their own ideas along with yours. Who, after that concepting, were the only ones to go and pitch all the work to the client. And, lo and behold, got their idea bought. We've all had the thought, "Why the hell do they need more work in their portfolio when we, as young creatives, are the ones who truly need new work as our creative career currency?" (Well, we didn't always say it so concisely and expletive-free.)

WHAT THEY SAID, summarized:

- Remember the importance of being a mentor.
- Share the limelight with others.
- Allow people to find their way.
- Discover the satisfaction in helping others experience success.
- Put aside ego and insecurity.
- Leave the work (and the potential glory) to the workers.

DON'T MANAGE

MANAGE PEOPLE

DON'T MANAGE
DEPARTMENTS.
MANAGE PEOPLE.

Maria is an ambitious go-getter who wants you to stay out of her way so she can get the job done. Frank wants as much face time with you as possible sometimes to a fault. Eric is incredibly talented when he applies himself, but has trouble staying focused. Vincent doesn't trust a word you say while Emily is your biggest fan. This is a creative department—a collection of unique individuals with different personalities, motivations, work styles, maturity levels, and goals. There is no single mold for a creative person, and thus no simple way to manage a department full of them. It's important to respect and understand their differences, as well as the preconceptions they have about managers.

Creative people aren't all cut from the same cloth. They have varying levels of maturity and sensitivity. They have different approaches to work. And they're each motivated by different things. Managing people is about being aware of their singular personalities. It's also about empathy and adaptability, and knowing how the things you do and say will be interpreted and adapting accordingly. Who you are and what you say may not be the same from one person to the next. For instance, if you're asking someone to work a second weekend in a row, or telling them they aren't getting that deserved promotion just yet, you need to bear in mind the individual. Vincent will have a very different reaction to the news than Emily, and they will each be more receptive to the news if it's bundled with different things. (Perhaps that promotion news will land easier if Vincent's given a few extra vacation days for the holidays, while you can promise Emily a bigger promotion a year from now.) Consider each person's myriad positive and negative personality traits, their life circumstances, and their mindset in the moment when deciding what to say and how to say it. Personal connection, compassion, and an individualized management style are key to coaxing consistent, rock star–level work out of everyone.

Being a leader also means listening to people's frustrations, concerns, ambitions, and goals, and trying to act on them as best you can. Maybe they hate their workspace or want a new partner. Maybe they're dealing with the insecurities and anxieties of working remotely. Maybe they're hoping to get more plum assignments, which could be seen as a vote of confidence in their abilities. Or, maybe they want a lighter workload. Hearing what they have to say and acting on it, especially before they have to plead their case or threaten to leave, is vital.

If you simply treat the department as a single entity, you're likely to alienate and anger some people, while missing opportunities to connect, motivate, and incentivize others. And if you try to get people to conform to your work style and personality, while they may begrudgingly oblige, they will ultimately resent you for your lack of understanding.

• •

SUSAN HOFFMAN

Chairman, Wieden & Kennedy

WHEN I FIRST became a manager, I didn't understand that everyone is so *incredibly* different. You've got misfits. You've got rebels. You've got brats. You've got intellectuals. You've got babies. You've got *big* babies. There's no two alike, and they have to be treated and understood as individuals, and you've got to give a long leash to some people. You just do. And if you don't understand who they are and what they are, you'll never utilize them to their full capacity.

SCOTT MARDER

Executive Producer, *Rick and Morty*, *The Mick*, *It's Always Sunny in Philadelphia*

THERE'S A LOT of managing personalities in the writer's room. I get a fairly quick gist of who can take rejection and who can't. You can tell who doesn't care and will keep firing away with jokes, and with them you're able to be pretty honest and shoot things down without them being affected. You can also tell when someone is kind of skittish, and so you might be gentle about saying "no" in the room and make sure they don't feel singled out, then take them aside later and share a better approach.

It's very easy to get intimidated by a room, especially if you're a new person. You're basically putting together eight to twelve class clowns from around the country and hoping they have this magic together. Even though the upper-level, seasoned writers are expected to carry the weight, young writers are encouraged to contribute where they can. They're not expected to do much, but if you don't handle giving the right notes to a young person you can affect their self-confidence early, and they'll just shut down and let the big folks talk all the way through. It's a game of keeping everyone feeling like they're contributing and involved, and making sure the chemistry in the room is working the way you need it to.

I think I'm pretty good at reading the room and being present. But I'm making sure to manage everyone individually. They're being evaluated individually. They're being evaluated on if they're funny in the room, whether or not they can write a draft, whether they're helpful on set. Unfortunately I don't have the luxury to carry someone who isn't contributing, and at the end or midpoint of the season I might have to cut people. But I never fire someone unless I've had at least two conversations with them about where I feel like they're lacking and how they can improve. That way, if the firing does come, they've been prepared for it.

EMILY MCDOWELL

Founder, Creative Director, Emily McDowell & Friends; Author, *There Is No Good Card for This*

SOME PEOPLE LOVE change. They're inspired by it and get excited by something new. They get bored if they're not constantly learning new things, and need that kind of a challenge. And some people, who are equally good at their job, get freaked out by change. They feel a sense of safety and security in knowing exactly what they're doing, and when new stuff gets thrown at them it really rattles them and makes them uncomfortable. Those two people are incredibly valuable, and could do equally amazing jobs, but the way you would approach them on a new project with either of them is completely different.

DAVID OYELOWO

Actor, *Selma*; Producer, *Come Away*; Director, *The Water Man*

THERE'S A FINE line between being a facilitator and a dictator. To facilitate you need a high level of emotional intelligence because it requires meeting everyone's needs differently. You can't have a catch-all mentality. You need to imbibe the unique stimulus coming off each person. Are they having a bad day? Are they a shy person? Are they an extrovert? Are they someone who thrives off encouragement? Are they someone who likes being left alone? Are they someone who works better in groups? Pairs? I genuinely think that knowing the differences between people and tailoring your management around them is imperative.

SHANNON WASHINGTON

Group Executive Creative Director, R/GA

I'VE BEEN A therapist, a detox buddy, a shoulder to cry on, and a peacemaker. My conflict-resolution skills have gotten really good because I'm dealing with creative people, some of whom still have some growing up to do, and who are extremely vulnerable. In order to get the best creative material out of someone, you have to help them unpack the bad stuff and help them get to the good stuff. And you have to create the most positive environment possible for them to do their best work.

BRIAN MILLER

Creative Director, The Walt Disney Company/ Global Marketing

IT'S NEARLY IDENTICAL to parenting several kids. Despite being exposed to exactly the same input and having been given the same success criteria, they approach it all in completely different ways and with different work ethics. The most fair thing to do is direct them with their own unique personalities at heart. It's frustrating because, yes, it takes a lot more energy and presence of mind to do that as opposed to a blanket, boilerplate, one-size-fits-all system. But once you see the connection and, ultimately, success, it's rewarding in the most profound ways.

WHAT THEY SAID, summarized:

- Creative groups consist of many types of people, personalities, and work ethics.
- Consider the impact of what you say on someone and how it might affect performance.
- Remember that what you say can be interpreted differently by different people.
- Tailor your management style to the individual.
- Having more personal relationships may improve your team's performance.
- Investing in each employee takes more effort but can be more rewarding.

REMEMBER THE FEELING

REMEMBER
THE FEELING.

Call me assumptive, but none of us started our careers as a manager or leader. It took many years of valuable on-the-job experience and learning to become the accomplished genius you are today. Along the way you made mistakes, you grew more confident, you pushed past your insecurities and fears, and you got better at your job. And now that wealth of knowledge and experiences that you've accumulated is going to be a great tool in managing your team. Because whatever happens to them now probably once happened to you before, and remembering how you felt in their current situations is going to help you relate with them and speak to their issues.

A good memory can make us all better managers. Recalling how you felt in professional situations, both good and bad, and then carrying that understanding with you, will help you to better empathize and sympathize with people as they face similar circumstances. It could be as simple as remembering the anxiety you felt as a young employee when you walked into your supervisor's office to present your ideas. Or remembering the dread you felt when you heard there were going to be layoffs. Or the disappointment when an idea you really loved was killed. Remembering how you felt when you were in their shoes in similar situations, and having it be the basis of how you make tough decisions, deliver difficult news, or give feedback is a wise thing to do. And it shows that you care about the folks working for you.

Today's leaders draw on experience and empathy to make decisions. They remember that they were once in the shoes of the people they now lead. And because they're able to use their past to relate to people, they know the potential impact of their words, actions, and a massively overblown tirade (which hopefully stops the massively overblown tirade from ever happening), and be a better leader because of it.

• •

AVA DUVERNAY

Executive Producer, *Queen Sugar*;
Director, *When They See Us, Selma, A Wrinkle in Time*

THE VERY STRUCTURE and collaborative nature of my work is to hold hands with other people. Now that doesn't necessarily mean that my imagination or artistic practice is going to translate into good leadership. I think it's an interrogation of what the term *good leadership* means, and for me it was important early on to redefine that for myself as a black woman. Leadership didn't need to look the same way for me as it did for white men. It was okay for my leadership to be more maternal, more eye-to-eye, more emotional. I think artists are scolded for some of those things, but I think they're really beautiful leadership qualities when applied appropriately. The sensitivity to know how to structure things, to intuit how people might feel about a certain aspect of your direction before you even say it, to be able to shape things so that people feel like they're a part of it . . . these are things that require some imagination but always, at its core, a beating heart and a

warmth of spirit. These are things that are the through line of so many artistic endeavors, which fit very nicely into a leadership role if we can redefine what good leadership is.

I recently had a situation in one of my writer's rooms where a newer showrunner assigned a young writer to proofread the work of a veteran writer. When I said to her, "Did you not think that was going to make that veteran writer feel bad?" she replied, "I was just trying to think about getting it done." It took me aback, but if you're working from a more intuitive, emotional place where you're in touch with people eye-to-eye and not just moving them around a chessboard, then you would be able to know that something like that is going to result in hurt feelings.

I believe most artists and creative people have a built-in empathy and a built-in sense of justice, through the sensitivity of seeing the world with an artist's eyes. And if we can be fearless enough to apply that beautiful place within us as creative people to the muscular definition of leadership, and to say there are soft places in leadership that we can lean into and that's okay, I think that we'll be much better off. The way I encourage the people I produce for, the way that I try to lead by example in that space, the way that I try to create room for people to lead with a softer side is all part of this, and part of who I am.

Now, that doesn't mean that I'm a pushover or unstructured, but I think there needs to be new habits, new definitions, and new paradigms for leadership. And we're beginning to see them in so many places, where it's incredibly successful, and it's really about trying to make this way of doing things more prominent than it is a majority of the time.

SUSAN CREDLE

Global Chief Creative Officer, FCB Global

THE FIRST PART of my career, I operated in a world of scarcity. "This might be the last great partner I have. This might be the last great client. This might be the last great brief. I'm only as good as my last great piece of work." I think, as a maker, scarcity is the way you often feel. In this mindset, on the front lines, you embrace a survival mode. It's an angst-ridden, paranoid place that probably exists at the bottom of Maslow's hierarchy of needs.

I found as a leader that I wasn't in a scarcity situation anymore. There was an abundance of talent that I could go to, an abundance of briefs I could get involved with, an abundance of opportunities coming in from different clients. And knowing what I knew about being in

scarcity mode, I became generous with my time, thinking, empathy, and support. The days when I feel like I've been generous with people are the days I can go home happy.

RON RADZINER

President, Design Partner, Marmol Radziner Architects

I THINK THAT I'm constantly trying to put myself back in the mindset of "what was I feeling when I was doing this." I think you have to do that. You have to figure out what's important to everyone and operate with that understanding.

For senior leaders, what's important to them is that they're respected. If I need to have a conversation with someone, I'm going to that senior-level manager first, not the creative person below them. Senior leaders need to be in a place of authority. You have to respect that they're running their group. I'll go to their desk first and start the conversation, and then bring in the people who are involved.

In a way, mid-level leaders are in the hardest place of all. They don't have complete control. They're managing their team, but they also have someone directing them. And to continue to have creative input themselves, they're looking for components of projects they can develop and not quite hand off entirely. I don't think it's easy, and I try to always keep that in mind.

• • •

TIM NUDD

Editor in Chief, Muse by Clio

WHEN I WAS a junior writer at *Adweek* many years ago, I was a true pain in the ass to deal with. I had a fairly major argument with one editor over a single word in my first published story, and more than a decade later I passive-aggressively (okay, probably just aggressively) told another editor to take my name off a feature I'd written after he had (I felt) butchered it with some heavy-handed cuts.

As I transitioned into an editing role, naturally I began to feel more empathy for the editors of the world—those who deal with the prima donna writers, who toil in service to someone else's byline, who make stories better without taking them over and obliterating the voice entirely.

I was lucky enough to have one editor in my career whom I cherished above all others. She knew I had my doubts—that I felt editors only damaged my stories—and dealt patiently with the perfectionist asshole in me. She managed to expertly cinch my stories into better shape, even when I thought they didn't need it. She improved every piece I gave her in small, surprising ways. She helped me get over myself.

Managing someone else's words is a more intimate business than we sometimes realize. My goal as an editor, even when a piece needs a lot of changes, is to keep the voice alive at all costs, to *not* change a line if I can help it. When I'm done, if the me of twenty years ago wouldn't feel devastated at the results, then I've done my job.

WHAT THEY SAID, summarized:

- Today's leaders employ empathy and emotion in their leadership style.
- Remembering how you felt helps to relate to people's current circumstances.
- Understanding and sympathy helps strengthen your personal connection to your team.
- Becoming a leader is an opportunity to examine your previous mistakes.

The delicate task

of killing babies

THE DELICATE TASK OF
KILLING BABIES.

Creative people put a ton of heart, energy, and hope into their creations. Their work is often in a fragile place when it's first born into the world, and their makers have a strong attachment to them—hence why ideas are often referred to as "babies." When it comes to evaluating people's work, and sometimes having to kill their "babies" (stay with the metaphor, people), it can be discouraging, especially if their work is quickly dismissed or greeted with ambivalence by their creative leaders. As a leader, you can have the best eye in the world and a long track record of awards and accolades to back up your expertise, but if you can't motivate a creative person to do the kind of work they're capable of, or aren't able to guide them in the right direction, the work is going to suffer and the people working for you will soon be putting their resumes back into circulation.

The feedback you give and how you give it is vitally important to the outcome of assignments and, longer term, the satisfaction of employees. True, rejection and criticism are part of the game, but leaders need to master the art of saying something sucks. Keep your feedback honest, thoughtful, and constructive. Be specific about what works and what doesn't, and avoid the "I'll know it when I see it" approach. If possible, balance the criticism with praise and consider the impact it might have on that person's self-confidence moving forward. It helps to map back to your overarching strategy and goals as you determine what's not working and develop a path forward. Stay positive and enthusiastic, and whenever possible praise people for what they've done right rather than focusing on where they failed. It may not surprise you to learn that, "Giving negative and hard-hitting feedback causes so much more damage to people because of how people's brains process information," according to Jen Ostrich of Ostrich Coaching, which is why many people choose to sandwich critique in between glowing praise.

Lastly, make sure your feedback is constant and consistent. There's nothing more frustrating than trying to hit a moving target. If they don't feel like they can make beautiful babies, or babies they know you'll love, they simply stop doing it. And don't save praise and compliments for the holiday party after you've thrown back a few vodka sodas. Creative heads go to dark places in the absence of information; they get insecure, doubt themselves, and wonder what they're doing wrong. A few words from their boss can do wonders to their frame of mind and the resulting work.

• •

MARC WEINSTOCK

President, Worldwide Marketing & Distribution,
Paramount Pictures

I ALWAYS SAY, "Lead with sweetness as opposed to vinegar." When I have to say no to an idea, I am hyper-sensitive to the fact that in some way you're stifling someone's creativity.

I always take into account who I'm giving the feedback to and their level of investment in the project. For instance, if we're launching a movie, the way I deliver feedback to agents, heads of studios, the media group, etc. might be very different. I might say no to a media person but I'll tell the creative team that's been hard at work on developing trailers for weeks, "I like where you're trying to go but it's not quite right." And if I'm giving feedback to the director, I keep in mind that this

is their baby, and is probably something they've been living with for a very long time. I have to be much more sensitive and thoughtful about how I approach any feedback in those situations.

SCOTT MARDER

Executive Producer, *Rick and Morty,*
The Mick, It's Always Sunny in Philadelphia

I THINK YOU have to be really delicate with people when it comes to killing their babies, because at the end of the day you want everyone to be as funny as possible in that writer's room. If you're making people feel self-conscious, or making them worry that their job is on the line, or that you're counting their jokes, then they're just not in it and they're not going to produce results. The challenge is trying to say no to things but still maximize everyone's comedic potential.

There's plenty of people out here in my position who have little regard for their writers. There are some shows that are run like boot camps, where people are always afraid they're going to be called out or humiliated. I think people want to feel like they're in a safe space and they can be as crazy as they want to be, and they're not going to be judged too hard for the crazy crap that comes out of their mouth.

I want my writers to know that when I kill an idea or change a script I'm doing it in the show's best interest, and I'm not an asshole about it. My golden rule is to be constructive rather than destructive. I think writers would love the draft they hand in to be their last draft and to have to never work on it again. But the truth is that most people never see anything finished. They're used to work being continuously changed or getting killed.

Honesty is really important, too. There are so many people that enter this industry and only get notes on their scripts from the friends they trust. But if their friends treat them with kid gloves, this person is never getting any better. I try to be as frank and transparent as possible.

This business is just so much rejection, from pitching your own shows to pitching jokes day-to-day. You tend to get things shot down way more than they get in. You need to have the gut to withstand a lot of rejection, regardless of how it's delivered.

CHRIS ORD

Executive Producer, *Covert Affairs*, *Containment*, *The Enemy Within*, *The Brave*, *Girls on the Bus*

YOU HEAR STORIES about writers crying every day because of contentious atmospheres that are brought on by the showrunners. That's never been how my partner Matt Corman and I do things. We take our jobs seriously, and that means being good to the people who work for us. We run a cooperative and giving writer's room. That starts by hiring nice people. We want to be sure they'll be supportive of other people and will try to keep the ideas flowing instead of just saying no and trying to shut things down.

We have one senior writer on our show who has this great way of motivating people. Instead of killing an idea, he'd say, "Let's let it suck for a while and then come back to it." Generally, after some time away from it, the person who had the idea is less resistant to seeing it change or watching it die, but at the same time, it allows the people running the room to look at it again with fresh eyes.

RACHEL SHUKERT

Co-Executive Producer, *GLOW*;
Executive Producer, *The Baby-Sitters Club*

THE NUMBER ONE most important skill is to be able to tell someone when they had a great idea. People really remember that and will think of you kindly. Being able to have the humility to tell someone they did a great job buys you something. And it gives you the ability to tell someone when it's not a great idea.

JAMIE REILLY

VP Global Creative, Vans

EVERYBODY THINKS THEIR own babies are cute, but mostly they look like Winston Churchill.

ANGUS WALL

Producer, *13th*; Editor, *The Girl with the Dragon Tattoo*, *The Social Network*; Founder, Rock Paper Scissors Editorial, A52, Elastic

DON'T REJECT PEOPLE. If you have to reject ideas, do it in a way that isn't personal to the people behind the ideas. The second you pass any judgment on individuals, you're screwed.

JENI BRITTON BAUER

Founder, Chief Creative Officer, Jeni's Ice Cream

NOTHING IS MORE frustrating to a team than when you don't give great feedback and people don't know what you want. Creative teams need to know what it takes to satisfy you.

I think it's really easy to default to "I'll know when it's right." But the better thing to do is to go back to the objective: "What do I want to say?" It's a process, but you have to be

specific. It's just such a frustrating thing, and I feel like when you frustrate the people who care so much about the work, it's not fair.

GUTO TERNI

Partner, Director, ROOF Animation Studio

IN MY STUDIO, you're dealing with people who are focused on really specific, intense tasks. They'll spend three days modeling a CGI hand and are obsessing over every little detail. For a short time, this becomes their life, so asking for change is tricky. They become emotionally attached to that thing.

You have to be delicate when you change something. You need to know and respect their process. And you need to care about the person making it. It's a combination of honesty and being mindful of their feelings. If they know that you're coming from a good place, I think they're more likely to understand.

DUNCAN MILNER

Former Global Creative President, Media Arts Lab, MAL For Good

I THINK YOUNG creatives often have a hard time understanding that it's an iterative process, and that things can be improved with other people's input or by going back to the drawing board. At Media Arts Lab, there was a saying: "If you come here, you have to fall in love with building sandcastles rather than the sandcastles themselves." You have to enjoy that process of building. The process with Apple is that things would constantly evolve, and they'd hardly ever end up in the form they were first presented in. Most of the time, they actually ended up better.

KRISTEN GROVE MØLLER

Creative Director, 72andSunny

BE HARD ON the work but nice to the people. Kill bad ideas fast, but don't kill people's spirits.

WHAT THEY SAID, summarized:

- Take people's feelings into account when giving feedback.
- Tailor your feedback to the individual. Take a more thoughtful approach to those more highly invested.
- Consider the effect of feedback on future job performance.
- Be honest and constructive in your feedback. Give people a path forward.
- Time away from an idea can reduce a person's attachment to it.
- Giving positive feedback buys you the ability to give negative feedback.
- Teach people to embrace the ideation process. Rejection can be a path to brilliance.
- Never make feedback personal.

MIRRORS
HELP REDUCE

BLIND SPOTS

MIRRORS
HELP REDUCE BLIND SPOTS.

People don't always see the consequences or realize the negative impacts of their actions and behavior. All of us have "blind spots"—things we don't see but others do. It's up to us as brilliant leaders to hold up a mirror tor our people to see and discover their blind spots. By doing so, they'll become more self-aware, understand the potential consequences of their behavior, and be mindful of their actions. Maybe it's telling someone they can't wear flip-flops to a client meeting, or that they shouldn't blare hip-hop music in their office, or letting them know it's not okay skip an important meeting so they can go to Coachella and livestream from a hot tub. (Unless, of course, it's a vacation that's already been approved—in that case, stream away!)

With honest, candid feedback that helps people understand their bad habits, unconscious biases, and weak spots, you'll inevitably cultivate better creative people. However, that feedback needs to be handled delicately, since it's easy to misinterpret. It's important to build your own self-awareness into the approach. Know the individual. Be as positive, appreciative, and encouraging as you can. And, as with everything, define a clear path to success.

· · ·

XANTHE WELLS

Senior Director, Global Executive Creative Director,
Devices & Services, Google

AT THE TAIL end of my tenure at a past agency, I remember my creative director finally said to me, "People used to complain about you like crazy, but we never told you about it because you were doing well and helping us win new business." That was shocking to me. They were letting me mess up on the people management part of my job and live in this strange, protected space because they wanted me to keep producing and didn't want to mess up my flow. But how can you get to the next level if you don't have an honest picture of yourself? Since no one told me about what I was doing, I didn't grow as a leader. Had they made me aware of my issues, I could have been a much more valuable asset.

I think a lot of creative leaders don't give feedback because they're worried about how someone is going to react to it, or how it might impact their work performance. They don't want to disrupt the goose that's laying the golden eggs or say something to a high-performing employee that may make them want to leave. They're not honest with people, which doesn't help anyone.

In my experience as a leader, feedback works. I've seen complete 180-degree turnarounds because of it. For instance, a while back, there was one woman on my team who was continually terrorizing people. She had a "take no prisoners" style and was doing anything to make sure the work turned out perfectly, which included making the people she collaborated with miserable. So I had an honest talk with her about it. She was really resistant to hearing the news at first but eventually listened, and even though it was never her intention to be aggressive with anyone, said she would change. After the feedback, she became a lot more collaborative and turned over a new leaf.

I think we also need to encourage the people who work for us to ask for feedback, too. People are often afraid of asking, "How am I doing?" because they don't want to open themselves up to what they might hear. I think we need to encourage people to ask the question, and in fairness to them, be as honest as possible in our responses.

TED PRICE

President and Founder, Insomniac Games

AROUND THE TIME *Resistance* came out in the early 2000s, I had been creative director on just about all of our titles. But I was also trying to function as CEO for the company *and* helping produce the games at the same time. In essence, I was a bottleneck. As a result, I wasn't able to make quick decisions on the games. Worse, I wasn't able to explain why I was making those decisions I did make. And I was ignoring a lot of the frustration people were feeling because of my inability to function as a creative leader. Fortunately, some "Insomniacs" spoke up and told me, "You suck at this. You need to step away and let someone else take the creative reins on these projects." I needed to hear that feedback for our company to grow and thrive.

Today, with multiple projects in production at any time, we have a far more effective structure, which allows us to produce games more efficiently *and* pay attention to what team members need individually. Every team member has a lead, and every lead has a department manager. As a result, there's always someone who's engaging in a one-on-one conversation with each person on a very regular basis—usually weekly or monthly. To ensure that everyone can keep track of those discussions, we have feedback sessions each trimester where we ask three questions: What's going well? What could be improved? And what's next? These questions elicit a lot of honest conversations. They also uncover problems that we can help team members work through.

Just as important, we allow team members to hold up mirrors to their leaders. We designed two-way sessions where team members can tell their leads or department managers how they can improve their performances.

WHAT THEY SAID, summarized:

- Giving and getting feedback is necessary for growth.
- Creating a consistent feedback loop helps people grow and companies thrive.
- Feedback gives people a better understanding of their strengths and weaknesses.
- Specific and honest feedback can have a positive effect on performance.
- Encourage people to voluntarily ask for feedback.
- Hold people accountable to acting on the feedback.
- Allow team members to evaluate leaders.

BE A STRONG

FOR PEOPLE & THEIR PROJECTS

BE A STRONG **ADVOCATE** FOR PEOPLE & THEIR PROJECTS.

Simply put: have people's backs. You're in the somewhat enviable position of being at the forefront of your group. Your title alone makes you someone that people listen to, and instantly adds street cred to what you have to say. You get to represent your group and, when the need arises, lobby for the work and the people who are making it. Be the loud, supportive voice the people on your team look for, whether you're building support for an idea or being an impenetrable human shield for their work.

Your role also allows you to represent the people who work for you amongst senior leadership. Let the folks at the top know when people on your team have done something great, or are all-stars that they should be aware of. The people at the tops of organizations aren't always able to see the specific contributions on projects, which makes you the obvious conduit. Spotlight the people who are kicking butt and help them get justly rewarded for it. Advocacy from the right person can make all the difference in someone's career.

There's no end to the loyalty if people know you have their backs, and that you're supportive of the work they do. Loyalty means people will stick around and give you their best, even when the work or salary isn't optimal. At the end of the day, the greatest leaders tend to have grateful teams.

JEFF GILES

Executive Editor, *Vanity Fair*;
Author, *The Edge of Everything*

WHEN I FIRST got to *Newsweek*, one of my first real stories was about Nirvana's follow-up to *Nevermind*. I wrote about how their record company, Geffen, didn't think their new album was commercial enough, and how they wanted it to be remixed. Obviously, the band had intentionally made it uncommercial because they had very mixed feelings about being so successful, so I wrote a story about that tension.

The record company was furious and took out a full page ad in *Billboard* in the form of a letter from the band saying I had misled people, I was the worst of the worst, and it was signed by Kurt Cobain, Dave Grohl, and Chris Novacelic. I was just twenty-seven years old and that was terrifying to me at the time. I felt very vulnerable outside the magazine because everyone was taking Nirvana's side and *Rolling Stone* was writing articles about my story, saying it was all lies. Before the letter ran, I remember being called into my editor-in-chief's office. He asked me a few questions and said something like, "Okay. Great. Don't worry. Nothing is going to happen to you."

I felt a ton of support. It was kind of like a parent role when Dad says, "It's gonna be okay." I liked the fact that his approach was, "I am not going to throw you under the bus for this. You're a valued part of this team and we trust you, not Geffen." That was really important.

Oh, and by the way, years later, there was a Nirvana biography that made it clear it was all true. Just saying.

MARQUIS AVERY

Creative Director, TikTok

IT'S IMPORTANT FOR anyone in a leadership role to advocate for their direct reports, simply by giving credit where it's due. I was fortunate to have previous bosses advocate for me early in my career. Receiving the proper credit for creative projects and ideas was a contributing factor in my career growth and job promotions, and having this experience early on groomed me to pay it forward as a leader. I find various ways to give my direct reports credit, whether in the form of an announcement in a meeting with key stakeholders or ensuring they're featured in the company newsletter. Bosses often fear giving credit to junior staff for projects, as they feel it may make them look inadequate at their job, when in actuality it's the complete opposite. Highlighting and giving credit for a team member's great ideas shows that you know how to recognize, hire, and retain top creative talent. And when you help the people on your team get noticed, you get noticed. Across your organization, by everyone from the top down.

● ● ●

DAVID OYELOWO

Actor, *Selma*; Producer, *Come Away*;
Director, *The Water Man*

I HAVE FOUND that with my success it's important to pull people along with you. As a black actor and director, and as someone with a very clear agenda when it comes to representation and what I want to see in the world, I am trying to create a place where the next person doesn't have to push as hard as I had to when I was coming up.

BRIAN MILLER

Creative Director, The Walt Disney Company/
Global Marketing

THE ADVERTISING AGENCY I work for has a mind-boggling amount of work, which means that the senior executives are seldom aware of individual examples of excellence. Having had to be my own advocate in the past with little help from my superiors, I make a point to let these senior executives know when a member of my team deserves to be recognized. It can be as simple as an email. I also keep running notes of successes and exemplary behavior so they can be noted at the end of the year.

When you don't practice this kind of advocacy, or when a junior creative's successes are taken and used to advance the career of their boss, it can create distrust and resentment—which rots the foundation of creative relationship.

ANGUS WALL

Producer, *13th*; Editor, *The Girl with the Dragon Tattoo*,
The Social Network; Founder, Rock Paper Scissors
Editorial, A52, Elastic

A BIG PART of your job is cheering people on to be successful. You can't get into your ego's attachment to anyone's work.

WHAT THEY SAID, summarized:

- People appreciate the support of their leaders.
- It's important to credit people for their achievements.
- Pull people up with you.
- Make it a point to recognize people on your team to senior leadership.
- Talented people want support and recognition. If they don't get it, they won't stick around.

SET REALISTIC EXPECTATIONS FOR YOUR TEAM

EVEN IF YOU HAVE IMPOSSIBLE EXPECTATIONS FOR YOURSELF

SET REALISTIC
EXPECTATIONS
FOR YOUR TEAM

(even if you have impossible expectations for yourself).

Some of us in the creative world have exceedingly high expectations for ourselves, so high that they're never quite achievable. For better or for worse, we're never totally satisfied with ourselves. It's okay to be overly critical about your own performance—it's probably a quality that helped contribute to your becoming the amazing leader you are—but you can't hold your creative department to the same impossible standards and unattainable goals. Regardless of what you've come to expect from yourself, you need to provide your creative team with clear, realistic goals when it comes to their own work, timelines, and job requirements.

Don't keep your team guessing with vague expectations. Be clear and definitive, and give them a guide to real, attainable success. They shouldn't be caught by surprise by what you say when they walk in to your office for a performance review or to talk about a project. They should already know if they've nailed it or missed the mark.

FYI, I think I could have done a better job writing this section. Yes, I have exceedingly high expectations for myself, too.

• • •

AVA DUVERNAY

Executive Producer, *Queen Sugar*;
Director, *When They See Us, Selma, A Wrinkle in Time*

I'VE NOTICED THAT people who are really driven to go, go, go like me sometimes don't have the most healthy work environments around them. As a leader, I'm learning that just because I want to work 24/7 doesn't mean that I get to demand that of everyone else. Everyone has to find their own level of investment. Just because working so much makes me happy isn't necessarily the healthiest thing for everyone else. I need to set parameters for the people I'm taking care of in the workplace, whether it's on set or in my office. You don't have to stay as late as I do. You don't have to work all weekend like me. I stop myself from sending emails on the weekend and basically write them out and put them in a special folder, so people get hit with a blitz of a hundred emails on Monday. But hey, at least I didn't send it on the weekend!

EMILY MCDOWELL

Founder, Creative Director, Emily McDowell & Friends;
Author, *There Is No Good Card for This*

IT'S REALLY IMPORTANT to me that my team doesn't work crazy hours, but that doesn't mean that I don't. For the first several years of owning my own business, I worked to the point of massive burnout that I'm still coming back from. I had insomnia, so I was working all the time. I would send my employees emails at 3:00 a.m. when I'd think of something. In my mind, they didn't need to worry about it until 9:00 a.m. when they came into work, and they only needed to worry about work between nine and six, but when the boss is setting the precedent of "I'm up in the middle of the night thinking about this and working on this," even if you're telling them not to worry about it, people are going to feel pressured to worry about it. So I learned to write that stuff down and to wait until the morning to send things.

You can't expect someone to do things at the rate you do them, or to be as thorough as you would be. Even if that person is the most brilliant, talented, most relied-on employee. Your company's work is in your creative DNA and five times easier for you to do. It's shorthand for you, versus being more like translation for any other person. The trick is finding someone that's innately good at it, but more specifically, finding someone where the work comes easy and isn't going to frustrate them. And if the person is talented, and it's still a frustrating experience for them, then you have to take a look at yourself. You have to ask, "Am I giving this person what they need to succeed? Am I managing them in a way that they respond to?"

• • •

CHRIS ORD

Executive Producer, *Covert Affairs, Containment, The Enemy Within, The Brave, Girls on the Bus*

THE THING THAT I have to remember is that everybody in that room wants to make the best version of your show. Most people are trying to do a great job at their job.

WHAT THEY SAID, summarized:

- Establish realistic expectations for your team.
- Consider the unrealistic expectations that your actions communicate to the team.
- Temper expectations when it comes to doing things "as good as you."
- Judge effort along with effectiveness.

☐ make

☑ failure

☐ an option

MAKE FAILURE
AN OPTION.

Greatness is tough to achieve when you play it safe. Brilliant ideas, especially the kind that seem impossible at face value, require brave thinking. However, the more ambitious the idea, the greater the risk, and thus the greater the chance of failure. And if failure isn't sanctioned, that could mean a lower raise, potentially being bypassed for a promotion, or losing your job. If you want people to come up with those "what-if, who-knows, never-been-done-before, holy-crap ideas" you have to be okay with them not working out as planned. If you want your team to do something unique and break through, you have to be okay with clients or intended audiences potentially balking.

Don't assume that people will be fearless on their own. While many talented creative people would argue that risk is necessary, no one is going to do a high dive into a tiny bucket of water if they don't have to. It's justifiable that someone who greatly values their position, who is familiar with the type of mediocre work their client typically buys, or knows what their creative leader will probably like is going to do safer, more familiar work that doesn't put them in potential peril and keeps the paychecks coming in. Ambition and bravery need to be sanctioned and communicated by leaders like you.

On top of this, you and your supervisors/holding company/board should be willing to fail, as well. If you're going to give permission to the people working for you to fail in their quest for next-level brilliance, *everyone* should be given that freedom, all the way up the ladder. When everyone accepts failure as a potential outcome, the whole team wins.

• •

JOE RUSSO

Executive Producer, *Community*; Director, *Avengers: Endgame*; Founder, Bullitt Productions

OUR GOAL IS to create an environment that nurtures and supports the vision of creators and gives them the freedom to experiment. This freedom comes from knowing they have mentors and strategic experts behind them who can act as a sounding board when needed.

RAVI NAIDOO

Founder, Design Indaba; CEO, Interactive Africa

I SPENT MOST of my adult life until my late twenties doing postgraduate research in physiology. I was doing scientific research, measuring fluxes in currents across channels in a cell. One of the lessons you learn is that failure is just a data point. You just mark it down and try again the next day. You come to grips with failure when it's that normalized. When I migrated over to the creative industry, I think that maybe behaviorally and attitudinally, I was able to bring that with me. I can actually shrug off failure fairly easily. It's just a data point to me. "Great, let's learn from it and move on."

I try to be reasonably understanding of failure, in the sense that I look at it as an experience that someone has been through, akin to having scuffed their knees after falling. When they pick themselves up, that's not the time to get rid of them. That person has just learned an immense lesson. Having just paid for them to get that education, it would be worthwhile to get some benefit from it. All of these constant bruises and scuffs are part of the total learning. Especially in the design world, which is all about prototyping and experimentation, you design by doing. Failure is actually embedded in the whole design process; it's standard operating procedure. There will be blood.

We [Design Indaba] built a terrace of houses at a squatter camp in Freedom Park, which is in Cape Town, South Africa. Real families live there, but the experiment, the expeditionary sortie, was really to look at new materiality, new typology, new economically efficient ways to give empathy and dignity to the people who lived there, and eventually open source it and make it public domain. We absolutely flunked on some of them, initially. Some materials didn't work. Some didn't pass flammability studies. Some didn't pass environmental standards. You're constantly experimenting, and at the end of the day, you bring across the threshold the most viable proposition. In that instance, you take the risk and you actually build it. Failure is absolutely part of our education.

SCOTT MARDER

Executive Producer, *Rick and Morty*,
The Mick, It's Always Sunny in Philadelphia

FOR YEARS, RISK was the name of the game at *Always Sunny in Philadelphia*. We've had to push things over the years, and we certainly weren't going to do that if we were being safe. Some of our craziest episodes came from joke runs that you would never think would get into an episode, and suddenly you find you're doing an episode about "kitten mittens." And that happens because no one was scared of what would happen if they said something stupid in the room.

DAVIS GUGGENHEIM

Producer and Director, *Deadwood, Melrose Place,
An Inconvenient Truth, Waiting for Superman,
It Might Get Loud*

FOR THE FIRST part of my career I was scared to make mistakes and I wouldn't do anything unless I thought it was a great idea, which is very limiting and often paralyzing. What I discovered over the years is that the flow of ideas is much more important than the "success" of ideas. What you're really looking for is "magic," and where and when that

comes, you never really know. The minute you give yourself permission to fail, you become more free and the creative opportunities reveal themselves.

It's really hard to work creatively in an environment where you feel like if you say something wrong, or say something that veers too far from center, that you'll be seen as dumb, judged, unsuccessful, or could potentially get fired. You need to feel comfortable messing up. Failure is sewn into the creative path. On any given day you'll have a hundred ideas, and ninety-five of them will be bad, four will be mediocre, and maybe, if you're lucky, one will be good. You're not going to find that really good idea if you don't indulge the other ninety-nine. I believe that the constant churn of ideas is what leads you to "magic."

At my studio, I try to create an environment where people can offer up ideas, good or bad. At meetings we try to have a free-form period where people have permission to throw out whatever they like. But this is a work in progress and it's really hard to do.

RACHEL SHUKERT

Co-Executive Producer, *GLOW*;
Executive Producer, *The Baby-Sitters Club*

YOU NEED TO feel an element of safety to get to that uninhibited place where you can be great and creative.

• • •

LANCE JENSEN

Chief Creative Officer, Hill Holliday

IT'S IMPORTANT TO make people feel comfortable saying dumb things in front of you and making mistakes. You need to provide sanctuary and give people the freedom to play.

DAVID OYELOWO

Actor, *Selma*; Producer, *Come Away*;
Director, *The Water Man*

FEAR OF FAILURE is something to be harnessed and used as fuel.

WHAT THEY SAID, summarized:

- It's important to give people the freedom to experiment.
- Failure is a great tool for teaching and learning.
- Failure is fuel.
- The flow of ideas can be more important than the quality of ideas.
- Not allowing failure can negatively affect a creative work environment.
- Risks are necessary. Some of the best work comes from taking risks.
- Feeling safe to take risks and experiment is necessary to doing the best work.
- You should have permission to fail, too.

THE BURDEN OF BAD NEWS

THE BURDEN OF
BAD NEWS.

Like it or not, we're going to be the bearers of bad news at some point or another. As part of our jobs, we're going to have to tell people their ideas aren't quite good enough, or that someone else's work was better than theirs, sometimes in a public forum full of their peers. Yikes. We may have to inform someone that they didn't get a job they wanted, or that they didn't get the promotion they expected, or that the raise they were counting on isn't going to happen just yet. Or ever. On occasion, we might even have to fire someone or let people go. And take it from someone who's been a creative leader for over a decade now: it never gets any easier. We have to do things that we know are going to disappoint people, hurt their feelings, erode their confidence, and, on occasion, negatively impact their lives. If you have a beating heart, this part of the job can't help but feel like a burden.

Rejection of ideas (or, as I referred to it earlier, "killing babies") is a consistent and unavoidable aspect of the creative world. Hearing "that idea wasn't quite good enough" or "I don't like it" from a creative director or client comes with the territory, and the thick skin that results is going to make people more resilient and better at their jobs in the long run. It will also help them become stronger arbiters of their own work, and make them better at discerning what's good and what's bad.

When you have to fire someone or let them go, try to be as honest and transparent as possible. You're not doing anyone any favors by putting the news through a filter, and your delivery won't make its effects any less painful. Callous as it may sound, you just have to rip off the Band-Aid and acknowledge that, at least for the short term, you're going to be the bad guy. No method of delivery is going to make the news palatable or preserve a friendly relationship. Be direct, but also be aware of the person and their individual situation. For some, it's merely an unfortunate setback, but for others it might be more life-altering. While some might easily dust themselves off, others might be more fearful, angry, or distraught. They may even point the finger back at you. If the person is open to hearing it, offer up any wisdom or support you may have. Try to build them up as much as you can and prepare them for the potential shame and uncertainty they're about to feel when they walk out of your office.

None of this is easy. But sadly, it's your cross to bear.

• •

RACHEL SHUKERT

Co-Executive Producer, *GLOW*;
Executive Producer, *The Baby-Sitters Club*

THERE'S AN EMOTIONAL intelligence to this that's tricky. I think you have to deliver bad news in a Mary Poppins "kind, but firm" sort of way. You're not looking to hurt feelings or be an asshole, but it doesn't help to tiptoe around what you need to say or delay the inevitable. People are much better at handling bad news than they are no news. Silence or uncertainty will just dial up the insecurity.

You can't be afraid to let people go when it's not working out. The truth is, just because you don't work out in one writer's room doesn't mean you won't work out in another. They each have their own dynamics; they're not easy places to work, and a lot of people have trouble functioning in that kind of environment. But you have to have a thick skin. Casualties are par for the course.

SAM BERGEN

Vice President, Global Brand Creative, Beats by Dr. Dre

NEVER MAKE ANY formal reorgs. It's more like, "Hey, for the next little while we're going to try this person doing this thing and kinda see how it works."

LANCE JENSEN

Chief Creative Officer, Hill Holliday

FOR ME, THE hardest part is letting people go. I take it very hard. It's all fun and games until you have to let people you respect and care about go.

In New York, if you get laid off, you just get off at a different subway stop. In Boston, where I am, if you get laid off, at a certain level, you're moving. And if you've got a kid who's a sophomore in high school and they don't want to move, it can be really difficult.

TED PRICE

President and Founder, Insomniac Games

NO ONE THAT I know enjoys delivering bad news. Unfortunately, that's a key part of being an effective leader. To foster growth, you have to be able to deliver constructive criticism honestly. All of us have room for improvement, and I think it's a leader's job to help their team members recognize where they can grow. In fact, I hear constantly that this is what team members really want from their leaders—they *want* to get better and they *want* the advice and support of their leaders to do so.

However, I think new leaders in particular often paint a far rosier picture than reality because they're scared they'll upset their team members with honest critiques. They don't want to say, "Your work isn't good enough—let's address that," or "You're missing deadlines—let's discuss why that is." Instead, they'll take the easy path and allow the team member to think they're doing great. This is not only a disservice to an underperforming team member but to the people around that team member. When someone isn't performing, the rest of the team has to pick up the slack. This often results in the loss of people who *are* performing.

EMILY MCDOWELL

Founder, Creative Director, Emily McDowell & Friends; Author, *There Is No Good Card for This*

ONE OF THE toughest things I've ever had to do was to lay off people from my company. The hardest thing is figuring out how to be transparent without being too honest. You don't want to stress people out. If your whole company knew every detail about what was going on, people would start spiraling. If you tell people we had a rough quarter, here's our numbers, here's what we're doing, the first place everyone will go is, "Am I getting fired? Will my job be safe?" And it makes sense—it's their security, it's their health insurance, it's what they do. They *should* make it about themselves.

The burden as a leader is that you have to put the company first. Before your own job, too. And that's really difficult for employees to understand, because it means having to sometimes let people, sometimes good people, go and having to make decisions they aren't always happy about. You want to give enough information so that people can sense what's going on and don't feel blindsided if something does end up happening.

And even if you tell some people "your job is safe," even if they like you and trust you, that's not going to prevent them from feeling like the company isn't stable and looking elsewhere.

SUSAN HOFFMAN

Chairman, Wieden & Kennedy

YOU HAVE TO accept what management is about, and that there are aspects that aren't easy. Sometimes you have to let people go. Sometimes you have to tell people their work isn't strong enough. Sometimes you have to motivate them to start over. I would love to know who's good at that because I certainly am not. I don't think it's easy.

WHAT THEY SAID, summarized:

- Be kind, yet firm when delivering bad news.
- Communication is key. Panic and insecurity rise in the absence of knowing.
- Try finding a positive way to spin bad news, if appropriate.
- While getting bad news is never easy, it can also be hard on the person who has to deliver it.
- An inability to deliver bad news can negatively affect others on the team.
- As a leader, you have a burden to put the company first.

If You Have a Bull in a
China Shop, Move the China

IF YOU HAVE A BULL IN A CHINA SHOP, MOVE THE CHINA.

f you have an ambitious, take-charge creative person in your group, adapt to their methods rather than trying to slow them down to conform to yours. There's a good chance a hungry "super maker" will do amazing things when given the opportunity, so it will pay off to nourish their enthusiasm and intensity. Give them the space, support, and means to bring their wild ideas to life, and remove any barriers that stand in their way. Oh, and make sure to shield them from bureaucracy, too—bureaucracy doesn't take too kindly to these folks.

While you give your overachiever room to create, protect the people in your group who aren't as aggressive or self-motivated from feeling threatened or getting trampled. You don't want to lose people because a super maker pushes too hard and leaves a wake of hurt feelings behind. Ultimately, the integrity of your company culture is important. Make sure you have the interests of everyone in your group at heart by respecting their differences in work styles. Just because one person wants to work weekends, burn the midnight oil, and sleep underneath their desk doesn't mean everyone has to.

Lastly, be sure that while you allow a super maker the freedom to push the envelope, you instill in them the importance of respect, maturity, and a sense of perspective. Let them know they need to play nice with their peers, and that it's not the end of the world if their work doesn't get picked or requires revisions. Ambition plus asshole is a toxic combination. At the end of the day, talented people need to be considerate and kind, too.

MARGARET JOHNSON

CCO and Partner, Goodby Silverstein & Partners

IN EVERY CREATIVE department, you need a few unconventional disruptors who will push the limits and get to ideas that are new and different and that make everyone question the way we've been doing things. It's these ideas that win awards and new clients.

But often some of the most creative people have the most volatile and emotional personalities. Hence the line "Here's to the crazy ones." Pair that personality type with a career in advertising, which is also unpredictable in nature, and it could make even the most sane person crazy.

So the challenge becomes this: How do you not suppress the ambitions of the bulls yet make sure they don't harm others? I don't believe in adapting a group to them—or in forcing the bulls to water down their approach so they can play nice with others. Instead, I do everything I can to create a space where they can work at full steam in their unconventional ways. In other words, create a bullpen; don't put them out to pasture.

SUSAN HOFFMAN

Chairman, Wieden & Kennedy

IF THE PERSON is talented enough to warrant the added effort and insulation, I go to the right people and say, "You have to let this person have some freedom and explore.

That's the way this person is. We have to let them do their thing." Then I think it's important to determine the kind of creative director these people need to work under to thrive.

Not everyone has the same blueprint. Maybe they're quiet. Maybe they're wild horses. It's important not to try and train them to be like all the other horses.

LANCE JENSEN

Chief Creative Officer, Hill Holliday

YOU NEED PEOPLE who are going to be okay with doing the daily work, but you also need people who are like Icarus and want to see how close they can fly to the sun. Of course, it's your job to make sure their wings don't burn.

MARGARET KEENE

Executive Creative Director, Mullen LA

IT'S A SLIPPERY slope, and assholes can ruin morale and take down a department you've spent months, maybe years, creating. The whole agency, as well as your clients, know when you're coddling someone because they're talented.

You can't hide a petulant creative and pay them royally to just sit in a corner and come up with ideas anymore. Our best people need to be so much more: wickedly talented; able to lead internally with strength and conviction; and able to create real, lasting relationships with clients. That's the expectation now, not just a bonus.

For the sake of everyone involved, try really hard to vet these people before they show up. Everyone in our industry knows who the tough ones are, so it's not difficult to know what you're getting into. Know that you've got to be a strong leader if you want to simultaneously get the most out of them, and get them to respect the process and the people.

• • •

MATTHEW WARD

Creative Director, Cinematic Director, Bungie Games

TYPICALLY, ANY PRODUCTION studio has two or three hotshots. Often, they sit in the corner, live off of caffeine, and get paid 10 to 15 percent more than other people in their positions. They create some of the most amazing things out there, so you want to give them space to do their thing, even if they're not contributing to the larger agency culture. But, if they have no connection or respect for the folks who are trying to steer the ship, or for the larger team, you're going to have trouble making forward progress . And the production as a whole could certainly suffer.

── WHAT THEY SAID, summarized: ──

- Creative departments need unconventional disruptors.
- Create space for them to thrive.
- Pair them with leaders who will help them achieve their goals.
- Remember that both ambitious and steadfast employees are valuable.
- People still need to be respectful and easy to work with. It's important not to coddle people who bring down morale or can't work with clients.

MAKE
MORE
YOUS.

This book isn't just a collection of wisdom for *you*, it's hopefully the first link in a long chain that will allow the people working for you to become effective leaders themselves. At the end of the day, an important measure of your success is the next wave of great creative leaders that you help to cultivate.

Where creative leadership generally fails is lack of proper training, or leaders teaching people the wrong way to do things (and, thus, dooming many of them to make the same mistakes years later). Once you're in a position of influence and authority, it's your opportunity to fashion the future leaders of your organization, and to teach them the right way to do things.

Beyond just being an important facet of your job, training people is vital so that when you're unavailable, or you move up in the organization, or you one day move on to that next gig, they can easily step in and succeed. Your employees are quite literally depending on you for this. They want the experience and, just like you, they want to get to that next level in their careers. As uncomfortable as it sounds, you need to make the next you just as good—if not better.

• • •

JAMIE REILLY

VP Global Creative, Vans

I WORKED AT one shop where the only people who ever presented work internally were the creative directors. Often the teams weren't even invited to the meetings with the executives. My partner at the time, Kevin Tenglin, saw that the junior teams never got any face time with the executives, and thus, weren't getting the chance to present work or learn any facets of leadership.

So we decided that we were going to switch it up, and we had one of our junior copywriters present all of the work in one of the meetings with the president of the agency. We had worked with her to get her scripts to a good place, but it was still a little bit scary. The president was temperamental and could be incredibly harsh. We figured we'd let her present and then we would play defense if there was static. (Never hang your team out to dry, by the way—I probably should have said that you need to be a decent human being up front, but it's the kind of thing you hope you don't have to say.) Mostly, we wanted the execs to see how hard she'd worked on this stuff, and we wanted to spotlight her contribution because she was awesome and wasn't getting credit.

She presented all the stuff, and I thought the meeting went pretty well: good conversations, no yelling, no need for us to jump in. As we were walking out, the president grabbed Kevin and me and asked us to sit down. Fuck.

Here it comes. He's going to tell us not to waste his time again or some other mean thing.

He said, "That's more words than she's said in the entire time she's worked here. She did a great job presenting. I really like how you two are mentoring the younger teams. We don't have enough of that here and it's really valuable to the agency. Keep it up."

That was not what I was expecting at all. Kevin and I ended up taking on mentorship roles where the new hires would intern with us for up to a year before they were released into the wild. And in many ways, it became a growth opportunity for us, too.

SUSAN CREDLE

Global Chief Creative Officer, FCB Global

TODAY IT'S A talent market. There's plenty of places to go. If they're not happy with how you're leading them, and they're not inspired by you, and they don't like how they're managed and don't feel like they're growing, they're not sticking around.

TED PRICE

President and Founder, Insomniac Games

I STRONGLY BELIEVE in leadership training. Until recently, I know I failed frequently in preparing Insomniacs to make the jump into leadership positions. I would assume that because someone is a good designer, programmer, or artist they could easily make the transition into a leadership position and instantly make a good manager. That is rarely the case.

We now employ training where we focus on softer skills like mentorship, career pathing, and conflict resolution. Those are skills that a lot of us assume we know how to do well before we're managers. But when we're faced with real-life situations, we tend to shy away from it because it's difficult. Today at Insomniac, we bring in outside trainers to help us look at things from a different perspective. We also do a lot of internal mentoring, where those of us who have been in leadership positions for longer will mentor younger leaders and help them resolve issues or give them constructive criticism on how they're doing things. For us, trying to figure out how creative leaders can be more effective is a never-ending journey.

WHAT THEY SAID, summarized:

- Leadership training is important.
- It's important to give people exposure and opportunities that will help them grow.
- Great talent wants to grow and be inspired.
- Consider exposing creative talent to senior leadership.
- Helping develop talent also reflects positively on you.
- If you lose, don't focus on people's developmental needs; they will leave.
- Focus on soft skills like mentorship, career pathing, and conflict resolution.

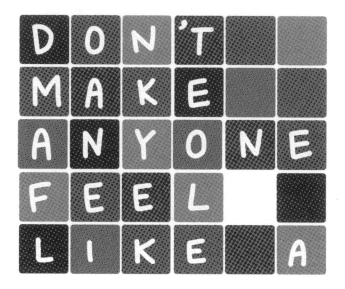

DON'T MAKE ANYONE FEEL LIKE A

YELLOW
STARBURST

DON'T MAKE ANYONE FEEL LIKE A YELLOW STARBURST.

Can we be honest? Nobody likes yellow Starbursts. They're simply there to fill up the package and brighten up the color palette. We all know that pink Starbursts are the best. End of story. Case closed.

But I'm not here to talk candy chews. I'm here to talk about the dangers of treating people who work for you *like* yellow Starbursts, the least favorite flavor of the bunch. When you play favorites at work, or make public your dislike for select individuals, you're creating a hostile environment, and that can be problematic for a number of reasons. For one, there are legal issues to consider. As a manager you can be liable for harassment when you show bias toward one of your employees. Your company can be sued, and you can be fired. But just in case that's not motivation enough to treat everyone fairly, bias can negatively impact the creative group dynamic. It can become divisive when people are jockeying to be one of their boss's favorites. If they feel like access to you is limited to an inner circle, or to the ambitious opportunists in the group, they may question your objectivity when it comes to the work, raises, and promotions, which could lead to resentment and a toxic work environment.

Creative leaders don't always play by the rules, so we're not always fans of strict corporate policies. In this case, we need to be. Universal respect and professionalism are mandates in today's work cultures, and based on your influential position, you need to be deferential to everyone who works for you, regardless of what you feel about them personally. Yes, we might have a yellow Starburst or two in our midst. And yes, we may have a few pink Starbursts we really appreciate and take a shine to. Regardless, it's important to treat every flavor the same.

• •

EZ BLAINE

Executive Creative Director, ChowNow

"**FIX YOUR ENERGY,** Ez." That's what I tell myself the second I start playing favorites.

I'm an addict for positive energy, which is why my team's happiness is so important to me. But I'm also interested in individuals: who they are, where they come from, what makes them tick. Early on in my management career, I gravitated toward certain colleagues. I thought they were great. But more importantly, I thought they were like me.

Now, looking back, I realize that the bonds I built with some were alienating to others. The inside jokes were just that: we were essentially roped off in an exclusive VIP area of a nightclub while everyone else looked on.

It was one of the hardest things for me to overcome as a manager, because it came so naturally. But eventually I developed a routine. I call it the "Wah Gwarn Check." ("Wah gwarn" is a Jamaican colloquialism that means, "What's up?" or, "What's good?") It's simple, and basically consists of daily status checks with my team. I ask broad, fun questions that don't always have to do with work,

and make sure I connect with every individual in a personal way.

Basically, I make sure the positive energy starts with me. That way everyone feels like a VIP.

DAVIS GUGGENHEIM

Producer and Director, *Deadwood, Melrose Place, An Inconvenient Truth, Waiting for Superman, It Might Get Loud*

I DON'T THINK anyone starts out trying to create a hostile work environment, other than sadists or maniacal power-hungry jerks. The problem is you can unintentionally create a hostile environment just by being more excited to hear from one person versus another, or by being dismissive of someone's idea, or by making what in the moment feels like a funny joke but ends up undermining someone in front of their peers. This is especially hard when you're the boss. I constantly forget that my words carry so much weight. I have to stop myself from instinctually doing and saying what comes to my mind because I don't want to create an environment where people feel less than anyone else. It's really hard to find the balance between having everyone speaking their mind but also not diminishing someone as an unintended consequence of that candor.

JEFF GILES

Executive Editor, *Vanity Fair*;
Author, *The Edge of Everything*

EVEN IF YOU don't want to be friends with the person, your staff is like a family. I try really hard not to play favorites. Of course my first choice is always going to be great work from someone who is collegial, whom everyone likes, and who is a complete team player. But creative people come in all kinds of different styles, and I'm used to working with eccentric staffs.

ROB SCHWARTZ

Chief Executive Officer at TBWA\CHIAT\DAY, New York

ONCE YOU PUT ideas over authorship, you get to a great place. Everyone feels like they're contributing. It's not agenda, worth, insecurities—none of those nasty bits. It's about the best idea.

WHAT THEY SAID, summarized:

- Focus on being inclusive.
- Favoring some people more than others will result in feelings of alienation.
- You can unintentionally create a hostile work environment through simple actions.
- Remember that because you're the boss, your words and actions carry more weight.
- Some people are going to be harder to connect with personally than others.
- Keep it just about the ideas. Specifically, finding the best ideas.

Make their struggle your struggle.

MAKE THEIR
STRUGGLE
YOUR STRUGGLE.

f you want to be a leader that people respect, admire, and love to work for, then remember this: whatever your team is going through, go through it with them. Leaders will engender far more loyalty from their teams when those teams realize that the leader's role doesn't grant them special privileges, but rather, certain responsibilities, which entail climbing into the trenches with their teams.

The sacrifices you make on behalf of your team become sacrifices they make for you later. By showing them that they come first and showing your willingness to work alongside them, they'll be more apt to do good by you, taking on those assignments that are less attractive, more time-consuming, or outside their normal scope of work. Empathy is the bedrock of loyalty. Perhaps your team is struggling with an assignment and needs help discovering more fruitful pathways. Or perhaps they're working day, night, and weekend to meet a deadline. Those are the moments when the organizational structure should collapse and, like a field general in battle, you should work shoulder-to-shoulder to get the job done.

I'm not suggesting that you solve your team's problems, or feed your own ego by doing the heavy lifting for them. You still need to give your team room to develop their own work so that they can grow, learn to problem-solve, and feel ownership over their projects rather than having you bear the burden every time. (Martyr complexes are, in general, annoying and a massive waste of your time.) It's definitely a fine line between resentment and appreciation. But a willingness to help, take on additional responsibility, and even share in your team's discomfort will lead to longer-term devotion. And let's not forget, it also leads to a better chance for your projects' success.

• •

SARAH MAY BATES

VP, Creative Director, RPA;
Director, Podcaster, Founder, Yay with Me

AS A CREATIVE director in advertising, it's important to have a producer's mindset. If you have a concept that your teams love but is impossible to bring to life, it's time to put on a few more hats. I ask everyone on my team, including those in other departments, how we can make something happen. Does anyone have any ideas? You have a nice camera, right? Let's shoot something with it. You can draw, right? Can you draw something for this project? Whether it's shooting something with my team over a weekend or mining my parents' basement for props, it's important (and rewarding) to get your hands dirty in the creative process. Make their problem your problem. How you conduct yourself in situations where there are few resources or severe limitations can be the most powerful lesson you teach your creatives.

I try to instill this in everyone who works on my team: you can do anything and you should, at the very least, try. Sometimes that means we're watching YouTube tutorials together. Sometimes that means we're setting up impromptu tabletop shoots. When you can make things with your teams and not bring your ego into it, they'll see you as a creative thinker and not a title. At the end of the day, that makes them more inspired to push their own creative boundaries.

Who you really are as leader is who you are when things aren't going well for your team. It's really important that they witness you as a person who will show up if shit's hitting the fan. Personally, I think there's something pretty wonderful that happens when you and your teams overcome a difficult project together. Your bonds deepen, your war stories grow even bigger, and your team's trust in you solidifies.

VALERIE VAN GALDER

CEO, Depressed Cake Shop;
Producer, former President of Marketing, Sony Pictures

I WANT THE people who work for me to feel like I'm part of the team, not like, "Here comes this marketing woman who's going to come in and squash me." I like to create *esprit de corps*. You need to have process and organization, but I also think you need to show up every day, and, when necessary, stuff envelopes on the floor with people (which I've done). I truly believe in "company and project first, self second."

TED PRICE

President and Founder, Insomniac Games

WHEN EVERYBODY IS participating in creating the games, there is the sense that we're all working together versus having a layer of management that is distant or disengaged. Obviously, we have artists and designers and sound designers who are creating assets, writing code, and making sure all the pieces are working together. But there are also many of us in leadership positions who are participating in the creative process in some fashion. Whether we're giving feedback on story and design, spending time playing the builds, or just talking to team members about what's going well and what isn't, we're engaged.

Those of us in leadership positions must take the time to understand what it is that we're making by playing and reviewing content. We need to be able to demonstrate to the rest of the team that we really do understand our designs *and* the constraints of production versus just saying bone-headed things like "Well, work faster!" Or "Can't you just cut that feature?" Plus, if we're doing our jobs right, we're also focusing on big-picture issues like communication blockages, pipeline breakdowns, and managing external partners. But we can't do that effectively unless we really understand what we're making

WHAT THEY SAID, summarized:

- Don't be afraid to get your hands dirty.
- Be willing to work on their behalf and to wear multiple hats.
- The things you do to help your team when things aren't going well will define you.
- Being engaged and available will help ingratiate you to your team.
- Company and project needs should come before your personal needs.
- Staying engaged in projects keeps you connected to the team and improves the creative product.

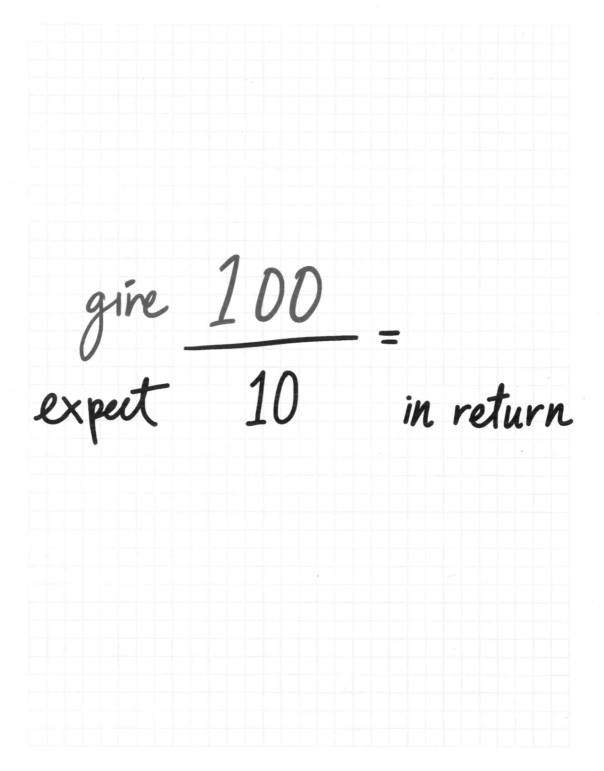

give $\dfrac{100}{10}$ = in return

expect

GIVE A HUNDRED.
EXPECT TEN IN
RETURN.

What goes around doesn't necessarily come back around. If you're hoping that the things you do on behalf of the people on your team will be met with tremendous appreciation or a deepened sense of loyalty, you might want to temper your expectations. I hate to piss on the campfire, but as much as we'd love for our sacrifices, support, and dedication to result in a massive debt of gratitude, that isn't usually the case. (Nor should it be.)

You're a creative leader, and while you may align yourself with the creative folks that you oversee and spend a considerable amount of your time and mental energy worrying about how you can help them, you are also management, and because of that you inspire a certain amount of caution and distrust among those who work for you. Another reason you shouldn't expect your team to echo your loyalty is the self-preservationist aspect of creativity. Given the fact that most fields of creativity are dog-eat-dog, many people are focused on their own ambitions and survival first and foremost. No offense to you, but if something comes along that improves their probability for awards, increases their salary, or guarantees longer-term job security, a creative professional will be hard-pressed to say, "I wish I could, but no."

To love a career in creative leadership is to embrace altruism. Know that you will be helping your people, and that you need to give without expectation of receiving. Help people build their careers, be a fierce defender and promoter of their work, lobby for them to get the raises and promotions they deserve, and celebrate that moment they come into your office and announce a big job somewhere else (while secretly biting your lip till it bleeds). It's all part of the job.

• •

EMILY MCDOWELL

Founder, Creative Director, Emily McDowell & Friends;
Author, *There Is No Good Card for This*

MY BUSINESS PARTNERS and I are always going out of our way to make our employees feel good. We give wherever we can. We try to make the office a fun place to work. We give them the freedom to work from home. We don't want people working past six thirty. Basically, we're always trying to figure out ways to make their lives better. But for some people it's never enough. It's like, "Oh great, you brought in a sound healer to do a sound bath for us, but it's at 4:00 p.m. and you should have done it at 3:00 p.m. because my day ends at 5:00 p.m. and now I'm going to have to be here an extra half hour."

It's tough to understand that people aren't necessarily going to be grateful for everything that you do and all the sacrifices you make. But I've realized that this comes with the territory of owning a company, and there's not much you can do about it. In fact, shortly after starting my company, I called Court Crandall, who owned an ad agency I worked at when I was younger, and apologized to him. At the time, they were struggling and doing everything they could to not go out of business, and here I was complaining about not getting free breakfast every day. I just didn't know, and I think employees just don't know, and you can't expect them to not want free breakfast just because you're worrying about how to pay them. I don't think employees get it, nor should they have to get it. It's not personal or about me. And I have to remember that.

ROB LADUCA

Executive Producer, *Mickey Mouse Clubhouse*; Effects Animator, *Star Wars: Episode VI—Return of the Jedi*

MOST PEOPLE STAY with me for a while. I haven't lost very many. But I'm always pushing people and saying, "Hey, look, if you find something that really interests you, you should go for it." I'm like a mother hen. I don't want to hold anyone back. I don't want people to follow their bliss. I won't hold it against them and, in fact, I'll check in with them every so often to make sure they're enjoying things. And, not surprisingly, several folks who left have since come back.

• • •

VALERIE VAN GALDER

CEO, Depressed Cake Shop; Producer, former President of Marketing, Sony Pictures

AS I GOT older, I realized that everyone is on their own journey. In one of my early jobs, there was a woman who worked for me who was so good at what she did and I was so invested in her. I tried everything in my power to let her know how valuable she was to me, but she didn't feel it. She went on a two-week vacation and then she quit. I took it so personally and didn't trust her after that. I was going to rehire her a few years later and I actually couldn't do it because I felt so personally betrayed. I had to learn that if someone is going to quit, you have to let them quit.

WHAT THEY SAID, summarized:

- Don't expect people to understand your burdens, appreciate your efforts, or to be as invested in the company as you.
- Invest in your team's personal success and happiness, regardless of reciprocation.
- The people working for you are likely to be loyal to themselves, first and foremost.
- As difficult as it may be, you can't take their actions and behavior personally.

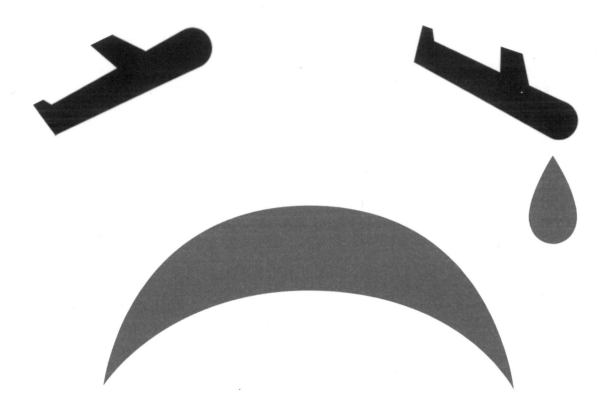

Don't take departures personally

DON'T TAKE
DEPARTURES
PERSONALLY.

"**D**o you have a minute to chat?" Here it comes: someone is about to leave. Unfortunately, that's just going to happen. Good people are going to find other jobs that promise them fame and fortune, or give them a shiny new title, or shorten their commute, or relocate them closer to their great aunt Susan who practically raised them, or they're just restless and need something new. They may go to a competitor, or start their own thing and become a competitor. They may even leave to take your position somewhere else. It happens and it's healthy.

Keep in mind, they're not necessarily leaving *you*; they're leaving your company. Though we may selfishly rue their choice, or get mad at them for not taking our very generous counteroffer or for not changing their minds after we told them how much we love and value them, try not to take it personally. Don't guilt or shun them as their tenure winds down, and definitely don't take umbrage. They may eventually boomerang back or become industry peers down the road, and you don't want your actions in the heat of the moment to mar a potentially valuable relationship.

You can keep your team happy by providing them with fulfilling work that whets their creative appetites, and by giving them opportunities to grow and develop their skills. But often, people will see that attractive new place and hear a recruiter say, "We think you're the most gifted person on the planet, and this new place is more amazing than where you're at, and you are going to thrive here," and they switch. In the face of those promises, the flattery, and the imagined potential, it's hard not to. And let's face it: talented young creative people aren't always mature decisionmakers. Those same traits that make them great at their creative jobs can sometimes lead to impulsive, irrational, regrettable decisions. They might not take everything into consideration when they make their choice, but we have to honor it. In the meantime, our job is to get the best out of them while they're working with us, and then to help them advance and move into the next part of their careers with success.

• •

ANGUS WALL

Producer, *13th*; Editor, *The Girl with the Dragon Tattoo*, *The Social Network*; Founder, Rock Paper Scissors Editorial, A52, Elastic

MANY PEOPLE HAVE stayed with the company for decades. That said, plenty of people come and go, too. I get it. People move on. People need things that can't be provided within the company so they need to grow. My feelings are going to be hurt, and it's going to sting really bad sometimes, but all you can really say is, "I'm sorry I can't give you what you want, but go do your thing. And please don't fuck us." When someone is leaving for the right reasons, you want them to go be successful and happy. And if they were great, you always want them to find their way back to you.

Sometimes people need to have a villain in order to leave a place. It's understandable, but it's tough to deal with. They clearly need to demonize someone, and that person is usually who they think is "management."

People generally tend leave the same way they came in. If they came in in a disruptive way, they're very likely going to leave in a disruptive way.

You have to have an open and naïve mind, yet still be guarded. While you hope that people will stay with you and take advantage of the opportunities and ability to grow and flourish, you have to understand that people have different ambitions and priorities. And if they're great, suitors will always be at their doorstep.

RON RADZINER

President, Design Partner, Marmol Radziner Architects

IF SOMEONE LEAVES to go to another city, for whatever reason, I totally understand it. If they leave to go start their own firm, I totally understand that, too. I did that. But if people leave to work for another firm in the city, and that place is good, I think, "Shit, what did we do wrong? Why did they leave us to go there?" and I try to figure out what made them want to go. Those departures are the ones that make me sad.

BRIAN MILLER

Creative Director, The Walt Disney Company/Global Marketing

I TRULY WANT what's best for the people on my team. If they can find what they need elsewhere, it's often because they are running *to* something, not *away* from us. If they are, then I try to use that as fuel to address these issues and make our place better. That sounds like Pollyanna BS, but it's true.

. . .

ALISON WATSON

Partner, Founder, Legacy House; Owner-President, Four Sisters Productions; former Director, Grind Studios

I KNOW THAT because I'm helping people grow in significant ways, they're going to want bigger and bigger challenges, and ultimately it will become a loss for my company. Mentorship is the most exciting thing for me to do, and yet, two of my last four interns launched their own companies with my help.

It's about finding people who click, but also about wanting them to have fruitful careers. One person I mentored, Dylan, loved music more than anything. He was super passionate and knowledgeable. I knew he'd be happy working for one of my clients at the time, Blackbox. So I sent him over there. He's now a VP and representing The Weeknd.

WHAT THEY SAID, summarized:

- Like it or not, people are going to leave.
- You're not going to be able to keep everyone happy. Or shelter talented people from suitors.
- It's natural to feel slighted, betrayed, angry, or sad when talented people leave.
- Introspection when people leave is important. Determine if they're running *to* something, or *away from* something, and why.
- If you truly value the people working for you, and there's an opportunity for them to grow or do what they love elsewhere, help them achieve it.

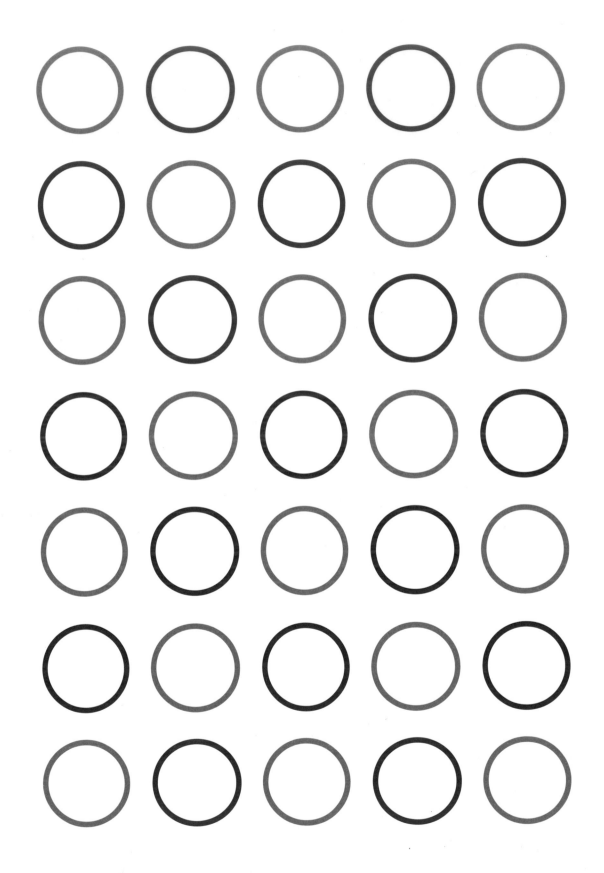

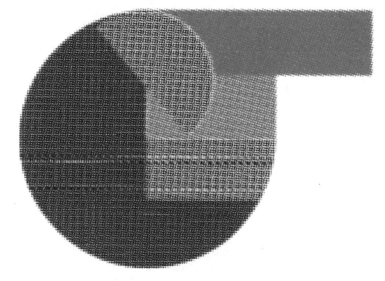

BEING A LEADER

SECTION 2
BEING A LEADER

Welcome to the front lines. You're playing an important and influential role on your team. Clients, supervisors, and those working below you are going to be reliant on your consistent wisdom, insight, and encouragement. "When it comes to leadership, you need to have a destination, and you need to be able to convince people to make the journey with you," says Jon Ikeda, Acura brand officer and former lead designer. And if that wasn't enough pressure, according to Sam Bergen, Beats by Dr. Dre Chief Creative Officer, "As a leader, the sole responsibility of the outcome sits on you, especially in a creative industry."

Depending on your level of creative leadership, your decisions could have huge implications on projects, staffing, revenue, and overall job satisfaction for many people. You're an important conduit between the work and the world, between your team and other teams, and between people's goals and achievements. You're also a focal point of people's attention, and according to Susan Credle, Global CCO at FCB Global, "The more power you have, the louder the megaphone you have. When you're at the bottom and you raise an eyebrow, no one really notices, but when you're at the top of a company and you raise an eyebrow, it makes headlines in the hallways."

Manifesting the emotional maturity and a fledgling ability to deal with the increases in responsibility, ownership, exposure, and scrutiny isn't easy. And there's a whole new set of soft skills that require developing, which, when honed to perfection, are art forms in themselves. Salesmanship. Mentorship. Diplomacy. Warfare. Motivational guidance. Facets of the new position require a different way of thinking. Your irrational brain, that endless spigot for creative ideas, diminishes in value as your rational duties start to increase. It's like spending a lifetime as an ocean-dweller and then suddenly being plopped onto land, where those glorious flippers that once propelled you through the water aren't nearly as useful anymore.

When I first took on the role of creative director, I didn't just instantly flip the switch and do all the right things. Far from it. I continued to approach any barrier to doing great work with a "knock 'em out of the way" mentality rather than working to mobilize support. And instead of trusting my uber-talented lieutenants to do their jobs, I let my personal insecurities get the best of me and continued to have a heavy influence on the work. It was only after seeing the resentment it inspired and losing a few talented people that I truly understood the pitfalls and nuances of my elevated role.

So . . . how do we adjust to our leadership positions? How do we handle the increased visibility and influence? How do we galvanize troops, build consensus, and bring out the best from people? How do we balance our passions for great work with the need for strong, trusting relationships with the people working for us? And how do we stay as happy as we were prior to making the move?

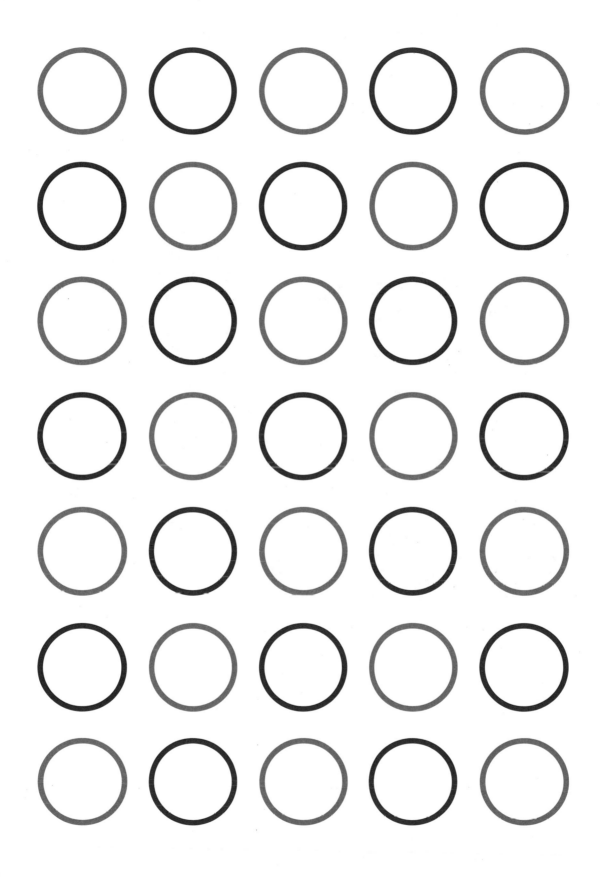

In battle, always start with the bluntest weapon.

IN BATTLE, ALWAYS START WITH THE **BLUNTEST** WEAPON.

No one wants a fight on their hands. But if a fight does happen to ensue, do your best to minimize the harmful effects and collateral damage. And remember that, as a leader, how you do battle is just as important as the fight itself. Pick your fights carefully, choose your weapons wisely, and consider the consequences of the skirmish. Are you alienating yourself? Are you putting your job in danger? Are you undermining your credibility? What are the long-term effects?

Let's be honest, we're passionate folks, so it's easy for us to get swept up in emotion, especially if it's regarding work we love. However, the scorched-earth, branch-in-the-beehive, "HULK SMASH!" tactic instantly puts the other person on the defensive. Rather than coming up with a solution, you become engaged in a battle, one that may escalate beyond the issue at hand. So close that nasty all-caps, reply-all, three-exclamation-marks-in-the-subject-line email and attempt to diffuse the situation in a more delicate, mature manner. Try starting with a reasonable conversation, alone and face-to-face if possible, where there's less chance of posturing in front of subordinates. Aim for reconciliation and, if need be, a certain degree of compromise. And don't go in hot, Maverick. Give yourself a few minutes to cool off and return to rational thought before entering the ring. Remember that a lot of what we do is dependent on relationships, so try to avoid ruining important ones in the heat of the moment.

CHRIS ORD

Executive Producer, *Covert Affairs*, *Containment*, *The Enemy Within*, *The Brave*, *Girls on the Bus*

WHEN THERE'S A difference of opinion on something with studio or network executives, our first plan of action is usually to determine the root of their issue, look for a solution, and make it a conversation. We try to reinterpret notes as best as possible and figure out *why* they might be having a problem. But occasionally, when we're at loggerheads about what to do, we borrow from dispute resolution methodology: "When you reach an impasse on which direction to take, look for a third way." Rather than make it a fight for their way or our way, we'll look for a third, unexplored way to solve issues. We'll explore a new idea and, generally, we get to a place that's even better than the first two without putting our relationships at risk.

BRIAN MILLER

Creative Director, The Walt Disney Company/ Global Marketing

I WILL FIGHT like hell (in a polite way) for my team when the situation warrants it. I also remind them of the old wisdom that states, "If you want to bring someone around to your point of view, start with their point of view." It's not manipulation so much as it's about understanding where the other person is coming from. It can only make the work better and smarter.

EMILY MCDOWELL

Founder, Creative Director, Emily McDowell & Friends; Author, *There Is No Good Card for This*

BEING A GREAT creative director means knowing what battles to pick and what to let go of. As a creative person, your whole stock in trade was to make things as great as possible and agonize over every little word and the point sizes of fonts, but you can't do that over someone else's work without making them feel terrible about themselves. If you nitpick every single thing, or dismember their work, your team starts to feel disempowered and undermined, and there's no trust on either side. So the trick is to either hire people that are smarter than you and that won't ever let you down, or figure out what to let go of so that people feel empowered. You need to really understand what customers are going to notice versus the minutiae that you notice, and determine what things you're going to push back on and have your creative people redo because it actually is going to make the work better in an obvious way.

MATT DRENIK

Creative Director, SOUTH Music and Sound Design; Recording Artist, El Camino Media, Sony Music Entertainment

IT'S MORE OF a long game than a short win. It's a fine line between getting what you want and being diplomatic. If I'm making a record and I know there are going to be battles in the process—everything from the songwriting to how the drums are recorded to the final mix—you have to pick and choose your battles. Overall, I'm looking at the album as the big piece, and there are going to be songs that you know people are going to gravitate toward, and that's where you fight.

WHAT THEY SAID, summarized:

- Determine what the issue is and make it a conversation.
- When you reach an impasse on what direction to take, consider a third way.
- Try to understand the other person's perspective.
- Determine which battles are worth fighting and which aren't worth it.
- Try to be diplomatic when going into battle.

GREATNESS NECESSITATES COMPROMISE

(sometimes)

GREATNESS NECESSITATES COMPROMISE.
(SOMETIMES.)

As artists, it's in our nature to fight for the sanctity of our great ideas. We're predisposed to protecting our work from those who might lobotomize the idea, or undermine our noble vision, or apply crippling amounts of logic, or—*gasp!*—put their superfluous stamp on it. We think the things we make should remain free of compromise. And, to a certain degree, we're right to defend them.

But it's not always that straightforward. Sometimes getting things made necessitates a degree of flexibility and, at the very least, a willingness to consider other perspectives. Creative projects often involve many parties, and each party comes in with a unique perspective. There may be times where, in order to get something made, you have to consider a change, legitimate or otherwise. Maybe the studio execs are willing to finance your film, but they're requiring it to have a PG-13 rating so that they can attract a broader audience (*legit*). They would also like to change it from a horror film to a musical (*not legit*) that stars one of their daughters who has two junior high school plays to her credit (*not legit*). Maybe your advertising client likes your commercial idea for their car but won't greenlight it unless it highlights the cost savings (*legit*), and instead of showing people driving it, they want to show a boxer driving it (*less legit*), and they want him to say, "They're knocking out high prices!" (*okay, kind of funny, but not legit*). Although the requests might change the creative product, in some cases we need to make them to bring them to life. In other places, a protest is understandable.

As much as it might pain you, try to be flexible and consider the concerns and opinions from everyone involved on projects, even non-creative people. There are times when a suggested change might vastly improve a project. Someone could suggest a line that makes your script funnier, or could point out a potential pitfall you didn't see. Heck, a person without a creative bone in their body could suggest a tweak to your idea that vaults it into masterpiece territory. Who knows? A great creative leader won't make it about them and get territorial. If it's a change for the better, it's a change worth making.

• •

MICHAEL LEJEUNE

Creative Director, Metro Los Angeles

SERVING AS THE in-house design studio for the nation's third-largest transit system is a daily exercise in compromise. If "nothing boring" is a key mantra, the flip side of that rallying cry is less of a flag-waver: "choose your battles." Our crew churns out some 2,500 individual projects each year, often more. Everything from maps, timetables, and customer app look-and-feel to campaigns for new routes, new modes (bikeshare), and new rail and highway projects moving from planning to construction. We do it all: photography, illustration, copywriting, and design for print, outdoor, small screens, vehicles, and wearable items. It's . . . a lot.

And the river must run, with each request bearing a different need, timeline, and deadline. At times, we still face stubborn colleagues and time crunches and a "let's just do it the way we did it last time" mentality that can be death to creativity. The solution? It's more of a compromise: Get this one out the door, with minimal change, or in the manner the partner wants, so that we can concentrate our creative energies on a project that needs more fuel. This does often feel like a compromise, but over time, designers have come to appreciate the levelheaded reality of this coping mechanism. After all, we don't have the luxury to pick and choose only the plum assignments. We've got to treat that hazardous spill poster with the same level of respect as we do our TV spots, because there's a passionate partner behind every request, and we're all on the same team.

So we build tools for compromise. We've created a good number of templated systems within our design standards in an attempt to hand over the keys to partners via Power-Points, MS Word docs, and writeable PDFs so that they can execute their own solutions when new design isn't needed. And we have also made peace with outside consultants taking over some of the day-to-day design we once were able to tackle ourselves.

As a creative leader, I made my peace early on with knowing that not all the work we do will get the same love or the same juice. Part of being in-house is seeing the whole forest, not just the trees. I measure our successes in bigger data, fiscal years, and overall trends. And by doing good, service-oriented work that design contests wouldn't look twice at, we carve out the time in our busy workflow for ideation and eventuality that is more exciting and rewarding. Plus, over time, I've seen something happening: partners who used to resist the unique and new, the "artsy" solution, the bold idea that feels too bold for their comfort level, are now asking for work that isn't safe, and is fresh. They see the big stuff, feel the effect, monitor the buzz of new campaign work, and then ask for that themselves. Compromise creates possibility.

SUSAN CREDLE

Global Chief Creative Officer, FCB Global

I REMEMBER A creative director group making something and they were fighting for every little detail and they were getting close to losing the entire project. And I said, "You've got an ice cream sundae and you're ready to throw it away because you didn't get it with sprinkles." I was trying to teach them when it was time to compromise. And of course that thing won a ton of awards and the team was like, "Thank you so much for not letting us shoot ourselves in the foot."

SAM BERGEN

Vice President, Global Brand Creative, Beats by Dr. Dre

YOU HAVE TO sell people on a vision about why you're doing something and a future value about why to do it, which has to be greater than the current value. For the most part, you have to build in concerns. But you can't build in *all* concerns because many people in the organization are comfortable with the status quo.

ROB LADUCA

Executive Producer, *Mickey Mouse Clubhouse*; Effects Animator, *Star Wars: Episode VI—Return of the Jedi*

I WAS MEETING with an executive who ran Disney Junior Channel, Nancy Kanter, about a project I was directing. She gave me very specific notes on a rough edit. I'm a firm believer that, whenever I get notes, it's worthwhile to explore them, because you never know if they'll improve the project. I know plenty of people who hate getting notes and will fight them tooth and nail, but I think it's worth considering any change that might make the project better. Who knows?

After doing the changes, I saw that they made the edit better, which I let her know. She said, "Thank you." That's when I found out that she had previously been a film editor for many years.

• • •

JONATHAN CAVENDISH

Producer, *Bridget Jones's Diary, Elizabeth: The Golden Age, Mowgli: Legend of the Jungle*; Founder, The Imaginarium Studios

BEING A PRODUCER is such a strange role. Every relationship is different. And you have to be really flexible. You can't go into productions with an unwavering view of what you want. You need to listen to everyone, because that's why you've hired them. They're brilliant at what they do. However, the key thing, and difference between being good at your job and being less so, is knowing the difference between what's good and what isn't.

In terms of directors, the best ones are flexible but know what they want. They're like magpies—they grab shiny things they see on the road and put them in their nest.

WHAT THEY SAID, summarized:

- Determine what should be open to compromise and what shouldn't.
- Compromise on certain elements may open people up to other things they normally wouldn't consider.
- Fighting for everything on projects can end up being detrimental.
- It's important not to build in concerns but not to compromise your vision.
- Explore people's suggestions. They might end up improving things rather than being a compromise.

align your spine

ALIGN
YOUR SPINE.

Your spine is the vital link among all the parts in your body, controlling the most serious of bodily functions and keeping you from toppling over. When the vertebrae in a spine are out of alignment, you can hardly move without serious pain. Everyday tasks become excruciatingly difficult. It's bad news. Now, let's go metaphorical with this: your team at work is no different. When your team members' goals and purpose are in perfect alignment, you're steady and productive. When they're not, you become much less effective, and your chances for success go down.

Teamwork matters. Great things happen when you surround yourself with people who share your same beliefs, passions, and whose talents complement your own. When you build a team that doesn't let ego, territorialism, or distrust cannibalize a positive work culture, good things happen. In an industry where it can sometimes take an army to make a single creative product, a tight-knit, balanced team of good humans plays a crucial role. Making sure everyone on the team is talented, supportive, and trustworthy is key to a healthy working dynamic, and is key to risk-taking and vulnerability, two important facets of creativity.

From the team that you manage to the bigger, broader team you work with, which is inclusive of management, it's important that you're all in alignment. And if not, well, there's no chiropractor that can correct things with a simple crack of the back. It might require something more dramatic. Like replacement.

JAMIE REILLY

VP Global Creative, Vans

EVEN JAMES BROWN, the Godfather of Soul, needed a kick-ass band to get down.

If you find yourself in the role of band leader, you need to get yourself a kick-ass band. One of the nice things about having the job you now have is that you get a say in who works for you. This is very big. You want to hire people who make you look good, like James Brown did. In your case, that means people who are smarter than you, think differently, know about different things, have different experiences, come from different backgrounds (both professional and cultural), and who are excited about doing great work. And you want to make sure that these folks' work excites you. You want stuff in their books to be stuff you wish you'd done.

When you're a creative director, your team is your extended brain. If you do it right, and you build your team right, you can have a broadly knowledgeable, nimble, and specialized brain. You can be both an expert at typography of El Lissitzky, the origins of the Mission School, know what the best examples are of the Philadelphia Sound, and also reference the newest trending behaviors on WeChat in Shanghai. Your team is the thing that will keep you relevant, and so they deserve a lot of your attention.

TARAS WAYNER

Chief Creative Officer, Saatchi & Saatchi

OBVIOUSLY, NOT EVERYONE will believe in what you believe. But the sooner you find the tribe of people that believe in the same thing, the sooner you will get to great work.

ANGUS WALL

Producer, *13th*; Editor, *The Girl with the Dragon Tattoo*, *The Social Network*; Founder, Rock Paper Scissors Editorial, A52, Elastic

THE REALIZATION THAT you can be creative but still be a leader is a great moment. But you can't do it alone. And you can't grow unless you have people around you that you can trust. You have to find people you get along with. That complement you, and vice versa. That you can communicate with and want to see every day. People that align with what your goals are as a company and as a human being. And most importantly: no assholes. Life is too short. Find people you can laugh with.

WHAT THEY SAID, summarized:

- Surround yourself with people who are smarter than you and complement your skills.
- It's important to assemble a team that believes in the same thing.
- You can't lead alone. A good team is important.
- Trust is extremely important.
- If at all possible, avoid working with jerks.

LEARN TO
DEPUTIZE.

You can't do it all, especially as you get higher and higher in organizations. As conductor and *Art of Possibility* author Benjamin Zander says, "Power is to empower." The best leaders surround themselves with talented deputies who can effectively manage in their stead. As much as you might want to handle it all yourself, it actually ends up hurting the work and frustrating the people who are making it. No one wants to wait forever for your feedback because your schedule is too packed, and no one wants to receive arbitrary or vague comments because you don't have the bandwidth to properly review things. No client or producer wants to have their timelines pushed because they have to wait for your plane to land, or for you to get out of six straight meetings. The best thing you can do for your people and your process is to have deputies step in and help.

The bigger your role in the company, the greater your responsibility. You'll be asked to oversee more projects, more people, and potentially manage more clients or new business pitches. Your time is more valuable. If you try to do it all, it will drive the people who work for you crazy—and it might drive you crazy, too. You need to decide what meetings truly matter, and what level of granularity requires your oversight. If you can leave it to a deputy to oversee certain things, particularly smaller-scale projects, you should, so that you're free to handle the bigger-picture, higher-stakes projects.

When you do deputize, you need to make sure that they feel empowered to make decisions. You don't want them to be scared that you're going to reverse whatever they say. And you should also make it clear to the people working beneath your deputies that your deputy is the ruling authority, and their opinions need to be respected. You want to avoid situations where teams bypass their deputized bosses and go straight to you with their thoughts.

Deputizing people not only frees you up to do more and play a more valuable role, but helps the people below you develop the leadership skills and confidence that are essential to their career growth. They'll learn to manage teams, oversee projects, and make decisions. And ultimately, if they're successful, they can start deputizing people of their own.

• •

SAM BERGEN

Vice President, Global Brand Creative, Beats by Dr. Dre

I LIKE TO give ownership, autonomy, and responsibility to my team. When anyone steps up and takes full ownership of something, I need to make them feel like they have the power to push the work to a place that's great. It's not about me.

I expect my creatives to behave like creative entrepreneurs. Everyone, no matter what, whether you're in studio pushing pixels for mechanicals, making campaigns, or building our website, you're going to behave like an entrepreneur and deliver excellence.

RACHEL SHUKERT

Co-Executive Producer, *GLOW*;
Executive Producer, *The Baby-Sitters Club*

THOUGH IT'S OFTEN with good intentions, many of us don't know anything but a "do it yourself" mentality. There's a lot of ego in that, and it's not useful in getting scripts out

every two weeks. Needing to be the savior is not anyone's best interest.

MIKE ALDERSON

Cofounder and Chief Creative Officer, Man vs. Machine

DELEGATION IS THE hardest thing for me. I'm still not there. Frankly, it's so hard because I think I'm better than everyone else. I might not be, but in situations where we have to get through something, I just take things over myself. Even though I want to give people autonomy, I have a hard time following through on it.

JOE RUSSO

Executive Producer, *Community*; Director, *Avengers: Endgame*; Founder, Bullitt Productions

YOU REALLY HAVE to delegate and place the right people in the right positions. You have to mentor and guide them but give them some autonomy.

BRIAN MILLER

Creative Director, The Walt Disney Company/
Global Marketing

THE CONSEQUENCE OF not deputizing people is to strip them of a desire to have a point of view about the work. When you know your POV isn't going to be validated or valued by micromanaging creative leaders, it makes you want to give up. It is truly castrating. I work hard to not be another needless, egomaniacal layer of approval.

JENI BRITTON BAUER

Founder, Chief Creative Officer, Jeni's Ice Cream

AT JENI'S, WE actually have a tenet we call, "Put your name on it." It's about empowering people and leaders to make a decision. They don't have to be right all the time, but they do have to have a point of view and own it. I love it when someone in the company just takes something on.

But it's tricky. For instance, we created a new recipe for waffle cones called the Buttercrisp Waffle Cone. It instantly started selling like crazy. It was insane. So our head of retail (who I love and adore) says, "No-brainer, we're doing a waffle bowl." The R&D team came up with a few options from the inspiration they found on the internet, but they looked like the giant taco bowls everyone else was making. I helped them understand the "why" behind what we did with the cone and then they were able to create a smaller mold and design. And now, wouldn't ya know it, it's selling like crazy, too!!

How much time was wasted doing that work, and where is the middle ground where people can have the autonomy to go off and make things and I only get involved when they're done? The last thing I want is to have everyone have to come to me before they can do something, because to be honest, most of the best things we've done as a company have nothing to do with me.

WHAT THEY SAID,
summarized:

- Allow your team ownership and autonomy on projects.
- Give people the opportunity to step up and deliver.
- Avoid the urge to do everything yourself.
- Delegation starts with putting the right people in the right positions.
- Balance mentorship and autonomy.
- Valuing different points of view begets different points of view.
- You need to find middle ground between autonomy and involvement. It's not always black and white.

Only apes throw their poop at people

ONLY APES THROW **THEIR POOP** AT PEOPLE.

So leave that to the primates and own your own shit. When things go wrong at work, don't deflect the blame onto others. You're not working in the mailroom anymore, and you're not a personal assistant doing latte and laundry runs for the boss. Part of being a mature leader is taking ownership of the good *and* the bad, especially any bad that you helped create.

It's important that you also take partial responsibility for your team's messes. When a sports team loses, you'll never hear the coach say, "Hey, man, I did a fantastic job. It's the players' faults. They're the ones who blew it." Why does this matter? Because when you throw the team under the bus, right or wrong, it tells the people working for you that you're looking out for number one and not for them. And if you're not going to have their backs, they're not going to have yours.

Consider the risk of not taking responsibility. There's the loss of trust from the people you work with, damaged relationships, and the reputation of not being a team player, which could follow you to future jobs. Be secure and self-aware enough to say, "My bad. Won't happen again." People will respect you a whole lot more for it.

• • •

SUSAN CREDLE

Global Chief Creative Officer, FCB Global

I THINK THE saying "Great leaders share credit and take the blame" is true. I think the reason they can absorb the blame is because they have a more confident place in the company (versus someone who feels more vulnerable). As a leader, you don't take care of yourself first, you take care of the team, and you have to put your own concerns aside and be the bigger individual. But it's a natural human tendency to figure out why something went wrong and want to feel like it didn't have something to do with you.

My natural default is responsibility. When we don't win a pitch for new business, I'm like, "I didn't do enough. I should have worked a relationship more. I knew that piece of film was okay, but it wasn't brilliant, and I should have pushed it." I think self-reflecting on the part you played, and constantly wondering about what you could have done better as a leader, is important. If you're blaming people, it takes you out of the equation, which means you're not learning. I prefer to be self-reflective and ask myself, "Okay, what part of this do I own? How could I have helped more?" You're going to learn something. And I believe that great leaders are constantly learning and constantly wondering, "How do I do it better today than I did it yesterday?"

ROB LADUCA

Executive Producer, *Mickey Mouse Clubhouse*; Effects Animator, *Star Wars: Episode VI—Return of the Jedi*

I NEVER WANTED to be the director or producer who would point his finger and say, "Oh, that was his fault," because it takes a village to do animated films and television shows. I never respected people who did that to their team. I observed that kind of stuff throughout the years and it never sat well with me.

Years ago, I was working on an animated project for Disney. They bought a studio in London to do the animation for it, but this group had yet to do a project for us. The studio said, "We're going to give them yours first and see how they do." Needless to say, they were having difficulties, and I ended up making an emergency trip to London. I walk into the studio, which was about sixty people, and asked to see all their work. I noticed that every single one of the Disney characters was off model, which in my world is sacrilege.

Rather than point a finger, I jumped in and said, "Let's fix this, guys." I couldn't blame them since they were acting without real guidance and just getting to know how things worked, and I didn't want them to lose their motivation. Instead, I made sure we fixed things together. The show worked out, and I actually ended up making a lot of new friends in the process.

VALERIE VAN GALDER

CEO, Depressed Cake Shop; Producer, former President of Marketing, Sony Pictures

I ACCEPT 100 percent responsibility when things go wrong. It's one of the things I take really seriously as a leader, and why I have so many successful teams. I always feel like it's my job to protect them and own every decision. When things don't go right, I always take the fall. And because I always act from a place of passion for the project and not myself, I've never gotten fired.

When I was doing the marketing for the movie *Snatch*, I remember saying to Jeff Blake (Sony Pictures Vice-Chairman), "Let me do this my way. The people at the studio are not my team, they don't like the way I do things, and I want to take the fall for my mistakes. If it doesn't work, you can fire me." Thankfully it did work, and I kept my job.

WHAT THEY SAID, summarized:

- It's important to share blame and responsibility.
- Taking responsibility for things is part of caring for and protecting your people.
- Sharing responsibility engenders loyalty. Not sharing it can result in a loss of respect and decreased motivation.
- Part of having a strong conviction is taking blame for when things go wrong.

Sometimes
you need to be a
**Benevolent
Dictator**

SOMETIMES YOU NEED TO BE A
BENEVOLENT DICTATOR.

f you ever feel a strong conviction about something, and no one is able to convince you otherwise, it's perfectly okay to leverage your leadership position (depending on how the hierarchy of your company operates) and say, "Thank you, everyone, for your opinions, but this is the way I think it needs to be." If, in your estimation, it's the best decision for the project or the situation, going a bit Mao is completely understandable.

That said, you should always make it a point to listen to people and entertain contradictory viewpoints. Things often improve with the addition of feedback, and the people that work with you should be encouraged to have and share their points of view, especially if it's in the spirit of improvement and not destruction. But sometimes you need to put the best practices aside and go with your gut, and in the politest way possible, make your dictatorial decree (knowing full well, of course, that you will shoulder most of the burden if you fail).

· · ·

JENI BRITTON BAUER

Founder, Chief Creative Officer, Jeni's Ice Cream

GREAT LEADERSHIP ISN'T coming in and saying, "Here's the decision. Now do this." It's about listening to people's opinions, which begins by making a place where everybody's input is heard and people's opinions count.

I've been in some very tough situations where there's a lot of good ideas and none of us are experts, and eventually I just have to make a choice. When there's a tough challenge or issue, I think a really good leader will just be decisive. You're going to make the best choice you can, but it may not always be the right one. If you're good and earning your position, most of the time it's correct, but there are going to be times when you're not.

It's not a perfect system, and I've learned the pitfalls. One time, after a decision of mine didn't work as planned, I had someone come up to me and say, "Well, I knew that would fail. I hated that from the beginning." That was because their idea was the one we didn't explore. That's when I realized I have to make an environment where everyone feels like they've been heard, regardless of who makes the final decision.

RON RADZINER

President, Design Partner, Marmol Radziner Architects

THERE ARE TIMES—MANY times a day, in fact—when I'm going to use my position as Design Partner to just say, "Let's do it this way." Someone has to keep pushing things forward, and with all the nuances and the many different ways we could approach things, someone has to step in and just make a final decision. It's not necessarily that one is right and one is wrong, or that my decision is always perfect, but someone has to decide. I have the perspective, having done this so long and so often. So I take the responsibility and say, "Okay, this is what we're going to do." Most of the time, we all get to that place together, but there are times when someone just has to decide. Generally, people are not upset by it. I think people just appreciate that someone made a decision and we can move forward.

BRIAN MILLER

Creative Director, The Walt Disney Company/ Global Marketing

THE IMPORTANT THING is to pick your fights. You can't do it too often or else you emasculate your team and make them less likely to go all in the next time if they think their creative urges and flights of fancy will just be usurped.

MIKE ALDERSON

Cofounder and Chief Creative Officer, Man vs. Machine

I DEFINITELY PREFER a strong, definitive leader versus a culture of messengers, or where power is sprinkled across a bunch of people who are all playing it safe and going home and saying, "Well, I didn't get fired today."

WHAT THEY SAID, summarized:

- People want to feel like they're being heard.
- Consider other opinions when making decisions.
- When people feel like they're being heard, they'll be more invested in the outcome.
- Regardless of opinions, sometimes it's necessary to step in and decide.
- Pick your fights. Strong-arming too much can emasculate and demotivate your team.
- A stronger, definitive leader can lead to stronger, unfiltered ideas.

BEING A LEADER

OPPOSITION

ATTRACTS

OPPOSITION
ATTRACTS.

When you listen to what people have to say, and give them the freedom to express their viewpoints (good or bad, right or wrong, contradictory to or consistent with your own), it can attract greatness on a number of levels. First and foremost, you get better ideas and insights through discourse. By inviting opinions, you'll identify pitfalls, discover unforeseen opportunities, and determine how to make a good idea even better. When you listen to people, you also attract more lucrative and disparate insights. By getting a diversity of perspectives from folks who might not normally express themselves instead of limiting your sounding board to senior people who are more likely to speak up, you'll get broader thinking that's more likely to accurately reflect your intended audience. And, lastly, you create an attractive growth opportunity for people when they're empowered to defend their work. By thinking critically and developing a stronger conviction for good ideas, they'll grow quicker than they would elsewhere and become better judges of good work.

Don't expect people to speak up or challenge you on their own. They'll naturally assume that contradicting their boss, especially in group situations, is a big no-no, so it's up to you to sanction it. Encourage people to share their viewpoints and maintain their conviction, or if you're so inclined, tell them you expect it. And when they do contradict you or call your feedback into question, you need to have the strength of character to brush away any reflexive insecurity, listen to what they have to say, and consider saying, "You know, you're right. Let's try your approach instead."

Of course, if you disagree with any of this, by all means let me know.

• •

ANGUS WALL

Producer, *13th*; Editor, *The Girl with the Dragon Tattoo*, *The Social Network*; Founder, Rock Paper Scissors Editorial, A52, Elastic

NONE OF US puts on a Superman cape, flies into a room, and solves a problem. Great managers aren't prisoners of their own belief system. If you're not rigid in your thinking, you can say, "Oh, that person has a really interesting point of view. It's completely different from mine, but it's a big value add."

The key is having a great team around you, and people who are willing to stand up for what they believe in and disagree with you. You have to create that atmosphere. You have to make it okay to clash, to disagree, to come up with crazy ideas that you could hate or love. Great ideas come from anywhere.

JENI BRITTON BAUER

Founder, Chief Creative Officer, Jeni's Ice Cream

I THINK OF our business as a fellowship, very much like Tolkien's *Fellowship of the Ring*. You're here because I want your opinion and you're a very necessary member of this team. I want your ideas on the table and I want you to challenge me. And I think that's something that you have to ask for and give permission to do because otherwise people won't. You have to hand people the freedom to do it if you're going to expect it from them.

MARC WEINSTOCK

President, Worldwide Marketing & Distribution, Paramount Pictures

I'VE SEEN PEOPLE say, "Do this and do that." I personally value everyone's opinion, and I want to hear from everyone. Senior people don't always love that.

SAM BERGEN

Vice President, Global Brand Creative, Beats by Dr. Dre

WHEN I CAME on board, I didn't come in and pretend to have the answers. This brand is ten years old. Besides treating some people poorly and the stories you hear in the industry when it comes to the work, they haven't done anything wrong. It's hard to come in and say, "I have all the answers."

The baseline of my engagement is: I don't have the answers. Instead of giving directions, I'd ask questions. I'd ask questions to get them to do explorations that maybe they hadn't thought about on their own. It left people feeling really empowered and invested in whatever solution we ended up going with. It was shocking for many of them how effective that was as a means of creative direction.

SUSAN HOFFMAN

Chairman, Wieden & Kennedy

THE POWER OF our individual voices has allowed Wieden & Kennedy to be slightly off-center. I love it when an account person challenges me on an idea. With strong arguments, debates, opinions, and different perspectives, the work only gets better.

WHAT THEY SAID, summarized:

- It's important to have people that are willing to stand up to you and challenge ideas.
- Create a culture where its acceptable to disagree.
- If people think they need permission to challenge you, they won't.
- Giving all opinions equal weight may create resentment among senior team members.
- Instead of giving directions, ask questions.
- Bringing together strong opinions and different perspectives allows for debate and benefits the work.

Bring out the human in people

BRING OUT
THE HUMAN
IN PEOPLE.

Nothing kills the creative spirit like a cold, corporate company culture. Guarded, distrustful groups that never quite get beyond the façade of "Happy Hump Day" euphemisms, in places that bear a resemblance to office-centric shows but carry none of the same irony, are more the norm than the exception. A few reasons for their existence are a lack of trust and a lack of respect. If people don't trust their employers or their coworkers, then they don't respect the roles of everyone in the organization.

Understanding that you're just one person and you can only do so much, make it your mission to infuse warmth, respect, and kindness into your management style. Try getting people to come out of their shells. Look for ways to connect with people personally, and to connect people with other people in the group on a more informal level. Try spending a few minutes conversing with meeting attendees about outside interests before getting down to business. And when members of your teams tell you their weekend plans, go so far as to remember to ask them how things went on Monday.

If people know that their leaders are as concerned about their workers as they are about their workers' work, they're more likely to let down their guard. And if there's a culture of respect at the center of companies, it will eventually radiate out to the other groups.

• • •

BRIAN KELLEY

Co-Executive Producer, *The Simpsons*

WORKING IN A comedy writer's room is inspiring. My hilarious coworkers create jokes out of thin air at breathtaking speed. If any discernible portion of this intellectual output were ever directed at making our show better, what television we could make! The thing is, what we mostly like to joke about is each other. It's not that we're trying to avoid work. We're not lazy.

All our oversharing and prying into one another's lives has a point: it's essential to the creative process. To illustrate, let me describe what much of our job looks like.

When we're trying to improve a script, our job is to identify places where there are no jokes, or bad jokes (I wrote those!), and put new, better jokes in there. We call these joke-free regions in the script "joke holes," because we've had thirty years to come up with the best term, and that's it. You fill joke holes by displaying them on a monitor, then having everyone stare at them for fifteen minutes in silence. You're usually working within tight constraints—"We need something for the church marquee, and everyone's confused about vaccines this episode, and also there's a blizzard, so all pitches should reference snow, God, and MMR timetables." Eventually, someone says something slightly funnier than what was there before, and we move down half a page to the next bad joke. (Hey, that one's mine, too!)

But the part of the job I really love comes much earlier in the process, when we're pitching ideas for new episodes and working together to map out how they'll unfold. That's when we put to use all the interpersonal knowledge we've built up over the years, because the best story ideas are invariably taken from our personal lives. Recently, a relative of mine discovered that her oldest friend, who organized their yearly vacation together, had, *for over a decade*, been overcharging their whole friend group so that her own trip was free. I only told this story to the room to get a laugh. But the great Matt Selman immediately said, "That's an episode." And, in early 2020, it was.

All because I wanted to waste a few minutes of my coworkers' time with a personal story.

CHUCK MONN

Executive Creative Director, TBWA\Media Arts Lab

EMPATHY + OPTIMISM + a well-timed coffee.

There's a lot of little things that go into keeping it real human-like around the workplace. Most of it is common sense if you grew up as a human. Here are three at the top of my list to help keep your team from turning into a bunch of lifeless corporate drones.

1) Have empathy. Most folks are swimming in the subjective sea of this business and are looking for reassurance that there will indeed

be land. For this, I love the fifteen-minute casual drop-in meeting. Just creatives talking out a problem with no expectations, comps, or pressure.

2) Be optimistic. If you're not having fun, no one will. Your mood has an effect on everyone around you. Usually, the crazier things get, the more positivity I put out there. When it gets really bad, I'm like a goddamn high school cheerleader twirling my team to victory. Convince folks that today is the day they change the world. It's the only way they will.

3) Make coffee, not outings. I always hated renting a bus and heading to a Thursday afternoon paintball tournament team-building thing. For most creative people, this just means "you're working this weekend." Instead, I prefer simple things, like just making some time to chat with a larger group of folks. I brought in an electric kettle and a Chemex to make coffee in the middle of the day. It cost about $50 and takes up about thirty minutes a day, but the effect it has is meaningful. It's akin to an artist stepping away from a painting to gain some perspective.

Also, don't be a jerk.

WHAT THEY SAID, summarized:

- Establishing a fun, relaxed atmosphere positively affects the work.
- Access and engagement with you offers people reassurance and opportunities to share their thoughts.
- Your mood and outlook is reflected by your team.
- Consider relationship-building events versus team-building events.
- Don't be a jerk.

Act Your

TITLE

ACT YOUR
TITLE.

One of the biggest hurdles for creative people to becoming strong, effective leaders is a lack of maturity. Nonsensical as it seems, our reward for doing great creative work is being given managerial jobs, which demand that we grow up and act responsibly. Thus far in our creative careers, we've been given permission to be less engaged, less mature, and less buttoned up than others in our organization, as long as it resulted in great work. If we showed up a to a meeting late? Never mind, that's just a typical creative person. We were unprepared for a presentation and left everyone to scramble and pick up the pieces? Well, that's a creative person for you. However, as a company leader, that behavior is no longer sanctioned.

It's time to grow up and act like your title. Be the mature, professional, reliable, and principled leader your organization requires. That means doing things like showing up to meetings on time, coming prepared, being organized, managing a calendar, being considerate of deadlines, communicating with team members, and reaching out for help when you need it instead of trying to handle everything yourself. And if all this stuff sounds unappealing or too daunting, there's nothing wrong with being a lifelong maker (see page 133).

• • •

SCOTT MARDER

Executive Producer, Rick and Morty,
The Mick, It's Always Sunny in Philadelphia

ON THE LAST show I was on, *The Mick*, I was lovingly referred to as "Daddy Marder" by my other writers because I was constantly taking on that role. I would walk through what we needed to accomplish, making all of the objectives clear. That would make everyone feel safe, like they could be creative because someone was taking care of everything for them. If I could earn their trust and guide things along, then everyone can just be funny, which is what their jobs are. And it allows us to make a funnier show faster.

Being a co-showrunner is a really tough job because you're sandwiched between the creator of the show, production, and the staff, and sometimes being that go-between can get a little hairy. The creator is feeling that added pressure because their name is on the show, and so the scripts pass through me but the buck stops with them. People are complaining that there's way too much to do for way too few people.

Some of the funniest people in this business were just class clowns that got their own shows in their early twenties and suddenly they're made CEOs of multimillion-dollar enterprises that they have no business running. There's no businessperson who is helping them run it. It's crazy.

There are just so many people in television who have so much creativity but don't have that other side of their brain to be on time, or have good awareness of everything going on in production. My job is to play that conductor that is hyperaware of where all the trains are in the station, in terms of knowing a script that's being broken, a script that's being written, a script that's being shot, and a script that's being edited, and on a network show those things overlap like crazy. I need to have one foot in the writer's room and one foot in the creator's room just to be sure everyone is efficient with their time. Most minds aren't remotely organized to handle that.

JONATHAN CAVENDISH

Producer, Bridget Jones's Diary, Elizabeth:
The Golden Age, Mowgli: Legend of the Jungle;
Founder, The Imaginarium Studios

BEING A PRODUCER isn't quite being a manager, but you do have to step in from time to time and become the responsible problem-solver when there are issues or the ship needs righting. Years ago, I was doing a big show in Northern Ireland about the history of the famine. We had to build a huge Irish village, so we sent out a huge crew of construction people to live out there. After a month or so and before any of the crew arrived to film, the local priest in the village asked to see me. He said, "I have to bring to your attention that a few individuals on your crew have been living untidy lives, and two of them have gotten two local girls pregnant." I remember thinking that four days of my life was spent sorting out these domestic problems in an Irish village, but that's the type of problem-solving you have to do when you're making a film or show. It's your role, no matter how peculiar the problems may be.

CHRIS ORD

Executive Producer, *Covert Affairs, Containment, The Enemy Within, The Brave, Girls on the Bus*

MY PARTNER MATT Corman and I sold our first show and instantly became the head writers and co-showrunners. Until then, we'd never been in a writer's room before. We had the advantage of having worked as a team for years, so we were familiar with a free exchange of ideas. And luckily, the Writer's Guild was offering the Showrunner Training Program on Saturdays. We would go there and learn all we could, and then on Monday morning we'd implement everything we took from the course.

SUSAN CREDLE

Global Chief Creative Officer, FCB Global

SOMETIMES WHAT HAPPENS is we don't have people behaving above us the way they should in that role. If you don't see your boss making a pivot as a manager and still behaving like they always have, why would *you* think it requires a pivot?

I think because there was less competition out there, and there weren't as many options for talent to go, people could lead a certain way that was dominant and aggressive, and they could dig their heels in on whatever they wanted. Today everything is about collaboration, and collaboration doesn't come with those attitudes that were prevalent twenty-five years ago. Nowadays, the leaders that are empathetic, collaborative, and that want the best for other people are going to be the most successful.

BRIAN MILLER

Creative Director, The Walt Disney Company/ Global Marketing

CREATIVE DIRECTORS WHO continue to act half their age are neither comforting nor cool. Truth be told, we're in an industry that has rampant, open, shameless, and despicable ageism, so I can see why some aren't that willing to lean into their obvious status as elders. But in the interest of modeling proper behavior (but not at the expense of creativity—the two are not mutually exclusive), I act my goddamned age and experience level. Sad that's a bold stance, but there it is. Let the chips fall where they may.

• • •

WHAT THEY SAID, summarized:

- Establish an environment where people feel safe.
- When people think they have a capable leader running things, it opens them up to be more creative.
- Leadership training is important. Especially since many creative leaders get their position based on creative merits.
- The things that are important to creative people today are collaboration, empathy, and an investment in their success.
- A senior title doesn't entitle you to be egotistical, immature, or overly aggressive.

HIGH-PAID PRIMA DONNAS MAKE PERFECT TARGETS $

HIGH-PAID
PRIMA DONNAS MAKE PERFECT TARGETS.

As you move further up the chain of command and your price tag goes up and up, the question presumably gets asked: Are you worth it? If you're someone who does great work, leads selflessly, doesn't steal people's pressed juice out of the fridge, it's an easy answer. But if you're difficult to work with, you may not be worth all the pain and suffering, especially if someone equally talented is out there and costs less. No one wants to work with a prima donna if they don't have to.

By virtue of our higher titles and years of maturation, many of us have grown out of our narcissistic and childish behavior. Over the years, we've seen the drawbacks of being confrontational and have become more solution-oriented. And we've developed a self-awareness of how our actions and etiquette are perceived by others. But there are still plenty of prima donnas in the creative world who believe that talent and tantrums go hand in hand, and their value to the company gives them the unique opportunity to be a complete asshole. Don't assume that your creative abilities provide you any special privilege or treatment. If you're a prima donna, the time will come when you will be asked to leave. And no one will be sad to see you go.

• • •

ANGUS WALL

Producer, *13th*; Editor, *The Girl with the Dragon Tattoo*, *The Social Network*; Founder, Rock Paper Scissors Editorial, A52, Elastic

EGO IS THE mind killer. Number one enemy. You need ego like you need saffron in a recipe: a little bit goes a really long way. Egotistic assholes come here and realize it's not a fertile environment. They realize they can't grow as an asshole, so they leave. They weed themselves out.

BARRY WEISS

Founder, President, RECORDS; former CEO, RCA/Jive Records; former Chairman, UMG East Coast Labels

NO MATTER HOW much talent you have, you're better off containing your ego. People with attitudes fall from grace. And when they don't make it, no one is sad to see them go.

You can't mistreat people and be difficult to work with. How many times have we seen someone flame out, never to be seen or heard from again? The people with big egos are far more prone to having that happen than others. You can have that attitude, and God knows how many in the music industry do have it, but there are consequences. What goes around comes around.

• • •

SAM OLIVER

Group Creative Director, Apple

I'VE KNOWN SOME prima donnas and I've heard stories about them, but I've been really fortunate that I haven't been around them much during my career. I worked at places where people like that didn't thrive. I grew up at a place called DDB in London where they had a strong philosophy in place—it wasn't just enough to be good, you had to be nice. And even though there were a lot of incredibly talented people there, they weren't ego driven, they would defer praise, they always gave me time, and they never talked down to me. That definitely stuck with me.

Maybe there's 0.2 percent of the world that is just so talented and so genius that you forgive them for being whatever they are because they're just so out-of-the-box brilliant, but the vast majority of us can't get away with that. From what I've seen, and as soon as those people are not doing brilliant work, they're not doing brilliantly *at* work, because they haven't built up any credence by being a nice person.

TED PRICE

President and Founder, Insomniac Games

AT INSOMNIAC GAMES we stated very early on that there are no divas allowed. We're very vocal about our belief that great ideas come from everyone. We make it clear when people interview that if you're not a team player, if you're trying to get your name in lights, Insomniac isn't the right destination. Over the years, we haven't been 100 percent successful in identifying those personalities during hiring. Yet we *have* been successful at ferreting out those folks pretty quickly after they join. They don't last.

In my opinion, one of the most telling signs that you're interviewing a diva is that they know very little about your company. They want to tell you all about what they have done and how amazing they are. But they can't name one of the games your company has created, or why each title is special. If I'm in an interview like that, I try to end it pretty quickly and let the person know they're just not going to be a good fit.

JONATHAN CAVENDISH

Producer, *Bridget Jones's Diary, Elizabeth: The Golden Age, Mowgli: Legend of the Jungle*; Founder, The Imaginarium Studios

I'VE WORKED WITH a lot of big directors. Very, very few of them are prima donnas. They might have a sense of their own importance but they're unbelievably professional. They tend to surround themselves with brilliant people so they're getting the best out of them. The prima donna directors I've been around have mostly been in the commercial world. And in film and television, it's mostly the executives who act that way. The commonality is that it's generally people who are dealing with a certain amount of frustration or pressure. They may be unhappy with their place in the pecking order, or insecure about their future, or are annoyed over having been commissioned for something and not having adequate control over it, and it manifests itself in really unprofessional ways.

When Andy (Serkis) and I started our company, we said we weren't going to work with people we don't like. Life is too short and we feel you can make good things with good people. Simple as that.

WHAT THEY SAID, summarized:

- A big ego won't survive in a healthy environment.
- People with big egos are more prone to misfortune, and don't often survive long term.
- When you mistreat others or are difficult to work with, you lose the support of your team.
- People become less tolerant of difficult behavior when the work isn't as great.
- While divas might raise the quality of work, they lower the quality of the workplace.
- Look out for signs of divas during interviews. Are they interested in the company or themselves?

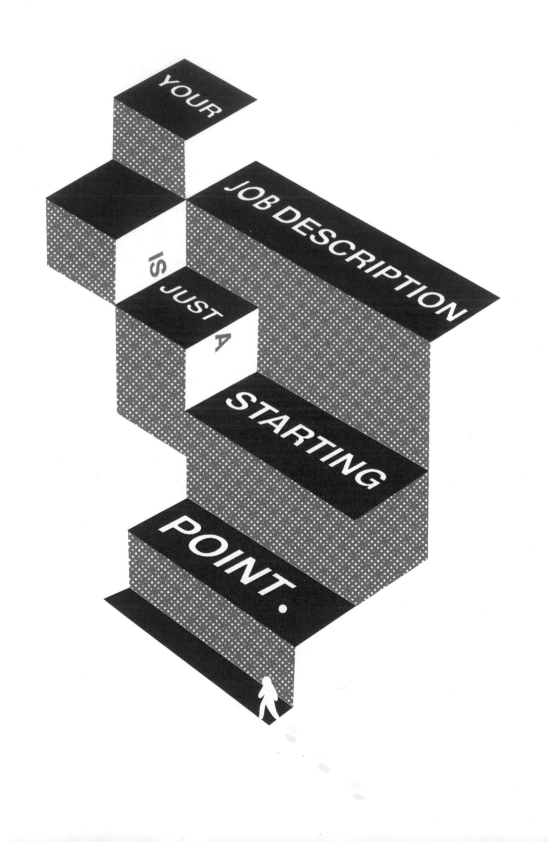

YOUR JOB DESCRIPTION IS JUST A STARTING POINT.

YOUR JOB DESCRIPTION IS JUST A STARTING POINT.

t's great to be valuable, but it's even better to be invaluable. Creative careers are competitive, and as your price tag rises, you'll need to prove your value to your company more and more. The more you can do, not just as a creative leader, but as a leader within your company, the better.

One way to build that value is to become a recognizable face for your company. Look for thought leadership opportunities that will help raise your company's profile and cache in the industry. Speak at conferences if you've got a knack for that sort of thing. Pen industry articles. Heck, write a better book about creative leadership than this one. Develop a social media persona where you can share your expert thoughts on your field. Or teach classes in the evening, which not only promotes your company but gives you a creative outlet and a pipeline for future talent. That's a win-win-win.

Another way to build value is to cultivate valuable relationships with people in your industry. Having direct lines of communication with the people in your industry that can promote your work or write glowing stories about your company will definitely increase your value. It also pays to connect with peers and influential types who may be able to provide future assistance and further your objectives down the road.

And let's not forget the value of deepening your commitment to your company. Get involved in things like cultural diversity initiatives. Or chair committees. Or join mentor groups. Or help develop best practices that make your company a better place to work. Don't roll your eyes at me. Those things matter, too.

ROB SCHWARTZ

Chief Executive Officer at TBWA\CHIAT\DAY, New York

I ALWAYS HAD this annoying thing in me that I have to be the person that no one can have a meeting without. I made sure to over-deliver because I wanted to be indispensable.

Making yourself indispensable, or crucial to the company culture, is a way to help cement your spot somewhere. By helping the company in ways that go above and beyond what everyone else is doing, you separate yourself from the folks who have the same title and same talent. Provide thought leadership. Play on the company softball or volleyball team. Ask for work, or make things in your downtime, instead of waiting for a request to land on your desk. And mentor young talent, simply because it's the right thing to do. Giving the impression that you're ambitious and hungry shows a selflessness that endears you to the place you work.

• • •

BRIAN MILLER

Creative Director, The Walt Disney Company/ Global Marketing

I HAVE SEEN some of the most cynical people in the world come to life when they believe they can actually help shape the culture in the workplace, whether it's through seemingly silly inter-agency competitions or even the smallest birthday celebration. It matters.

MATTHEW WARD

Creative Director, Cinematic Director, Bungie Games

COMMONLY, EVERYONE HAS a title and a pay grade and list of clearly defined foundational responsibilities that come with that—this helps build structure and accountability. But while those are things you need to do, there are things that are unspoken and encouraged. It's our job as leaders to make people aware of what they're expected to do and what they're being asked to do above and beyond that. I've known people who like to keep their heads down and just do their job, period, and I have to tell them that if they want to grow, they have to show the company they're interested in growth.

WHAT THEY SAID, summarized:

- Over-deliver so that you become indispensable.
- Find ways to integrate yourself into the company culture.
- Give the impression that you're hungry, ambitious, and selfless.
- People need to feel like they can shape workplace culture.
- When people feel like they can shape culture, they are more apt to.
- People need to know what they're expected to do *and* encouraged to do.

There is nothing wrong with being a lifelong maker.

THERE'S NOTHING WRONG **WITH BEING A** LIFELONG MAKER.

Creative leadership is not going to be the right fit for everyone. Not everyone is going to want to manage people, and truthfully, not everyone is going to be good at it. If creative leadership isn't your thing, then it's not your thing: Some people just get more joy out of making things. Some don't want to manage people or interface with clients. Some people would rather be in a room bouncing ideas off the wall or on the set of productions. Some are going to find out after making the transition. Some will know it's not for them ahead of time. Regardless, your career doesn't dead end if you decide not to move into management. In fact, it might actually save your job by not taking the position if you lack the discipline, temperament, or wherewithal to lead creative teams and projects.

An honest appraisal of why you want the job is essential. Are you doing it for the money? The title? Prestige? Because you feel like you have to? Or are you doing it because it's something you truly aspire to and appreciate the managerial aspects of a leadership position? Whether you're at the point where you have to decide, or if you've already accepted the position, determine for yourself what's going to make you happier—each and every day—in the short and long term. Consider if you'd even be good at the job. There are plenty of people who bypassed the management path because it wasn't where their talents lay, and remained makers until they retired, and loved their careers (and their lives) a whole lot more because of it.

MARC WEINSTOCK

President, Worldwide Marketing & Distribution,
Paramount Pictures

IT'S DIFFICULT WHEN someone is a manager but still wants to be a maker. It's hard for them to do the daily work of managing people. And it's hard to manage them, because on some level you're stifling their creativity by inserting yourself into the process too much. When leaders want to be in the back room making the sausage with everyone else, you have one of two options. You can remove them from that position, and rather than having them walk, pair them up with someone who can handle the leadership duties. Or you fire them. I've had to fire people who couldn't manage. They were really great creatives, but as leaders they were a detriment to the company.

SUSAN CREDLE

Global Chief Creative Officer, FCB Global

SOME PEOPLE WILL simply not want to do the job of creative director and will prefer to stay close to the work as a craftsperson. They're not going to be fulfilled by the management part. Sometimes it should be okay not to get into that management world. A great artist, a great craftsperson, a great doer, a great maker, a great front lines person, should be able to stay and be supported by their company.

At BBDO, there were a lot of superstars that really made work right up through the end of their careers. They managed a little bit, but there was definitely room for people to just make great creative. Over the years, I've seen that less and less. It feels like there's only one path: to get into management and client relationships. That does take a huge mental shift.

SUSAN HOFFMAN

Chairman, Wieden & Kennedy

I KNOW IT'S human nature to want to keep climbing up and getting the bigger title, but there are just some people who are better as creatives and should stay in this position. That's their super power. I remember promoting an art director to be a creative director and later we had to unpromote him. Management was not his strength. He's still one of the strongest, most senior art directors here. Some people think it's a failure if you don't move up. I say stick to your strengths.

WHAT THEY SAID, summarized:

- Not every creative person is going to be an effective manager.
- Not everyone will be fulfilled by a management role.
- Leaders can't make the work themselves and lead without stifling creativity.
- People need to understand that it's not a failure if they stay in a maker role.
- Consider allowing people the option of bypassing the typical promotional path.

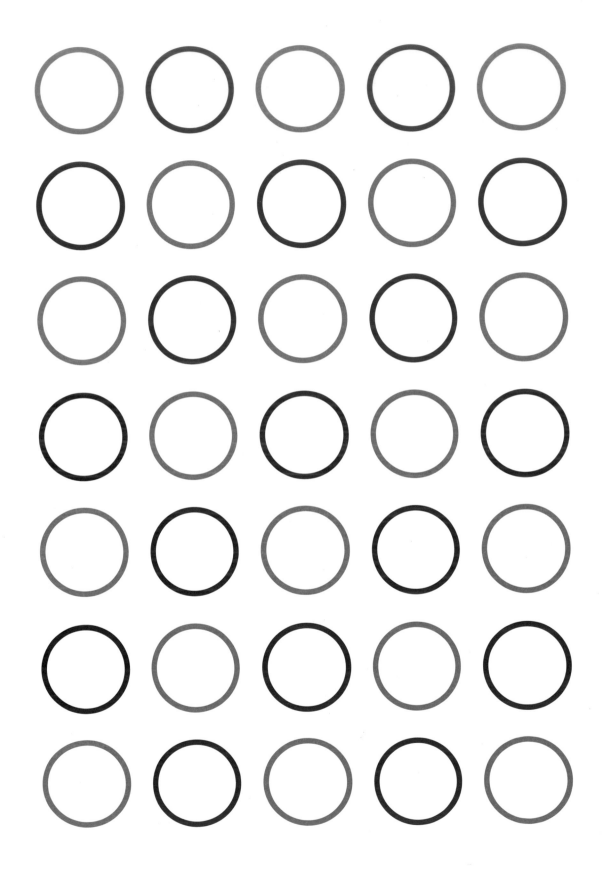

MANAGING CLIENTS
& HIGHER-UPS

SECTION 3
MANAGING CLIENTS & HIGHER-UPS

Thanks to your creative success, you've now established some valuable but tenuous relationships with people higher up in organizations, both within yours and potentially within your clients'. They're counting on you not just for great creative work but for steady, trustworthy leadership.

Thankfully, your new vantage point allows you to see more, hear more, and, ultimately, to do more. That means figuring out how to manage the many, sometimes incongruous, layers with varying motivations, and learning the subtle art of politics, diplomacy, and relationship-building. Says Bill Westbrook, former president and executive creative director at Fallon Worldwide and CEO of No Fences Consulting, "There will always be difficult clients. Your best strategy is to do everything you can to earn their trust."

This ascent into the ranks of management, the access to inside information, both good and bad, and the velvet-roped intimacy of client relationships is a new world for many of us, and a far cry from our isolationist maker days. This immersion demands an evolved perspective toward the work, and requires a precarious tightrope walk of being loyal to your team while still maintaining the best interests of clients and the company at large. The position is rife with risks and potential pitfalls, and you must learn to do things like read the room, know your audience, pick your battles, "respectfully" disagree, and find ways of convince people to do things they're not always comfortable with or amenable to.

When I first became a creative director, I couldn't help but feel like I didn't belong on the management team. In meetings I felt like an interloper, akin to Tom Hanks's childlike character in the movie *Big,* spouting wild ideas to a room full of disapproving executives (to be honest I'd much rather talk crazy toy ideas than financial stability). I had to work hard to establish myself as credible and mature, and show that even though I was wearing jeans and a T-shirt that said "Goonies Never Say Die," I was just as smart and insightful as everyone else in the room, if not more so.

I also had to deal with a creative group that, after I was promoted, became more guarded, resentful, and at times even contemptuous. I had to continually earn their trust and respect while pushing them to do great work, which is a tough balancing act. And I had to show that my privileged connection to managers and clients wasn't going to make me any less trustworthy or affect my allegiance to them.

How do you manage and maintain these relationships while managing and maintaining your own goals as a creative person? And what are the factors you should take into consideration when pitching, pushing, and pulling people out of their comfort zones?

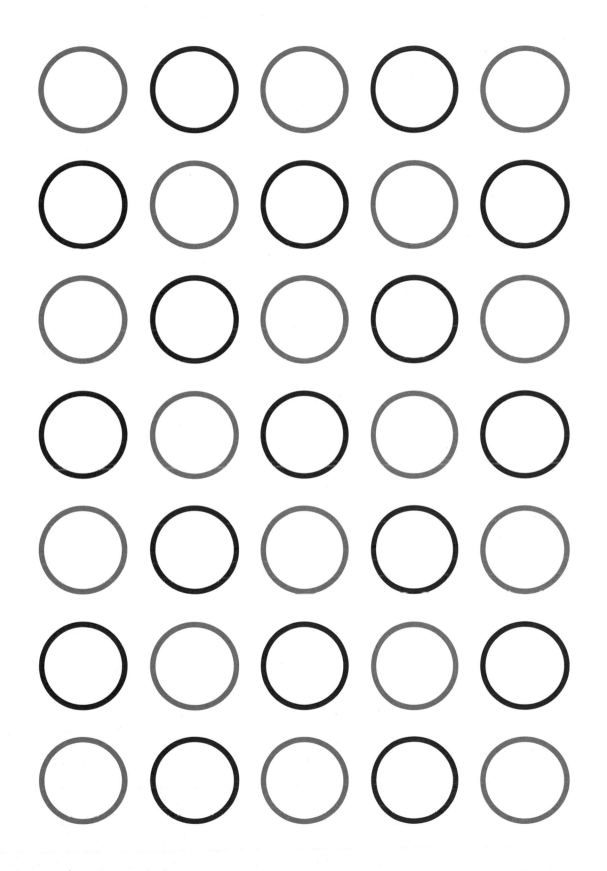

STRADDLE THE LINE BETWEEN

PARTNER

AND

PRODDER

STRADDLE THE LINE BETWEEN PARTNER AND **PRODDER.**

Pushing to get great things made while maintaining a strong bond with clients or supervisors is a tricky balance. You want that personal connection, but you also want the freedom to express yourself, debate, disagree, and occasionally pull people out of their comfort zones. Finding that balance is no easy feat.

That kind of relationship requires trust. People need to trust that you're pushing them for the right reasons and not selfish ones, which is why it's so important to build your rationales around how your work is going to help them reach their goals (and not how it's going to win you awards). Trust also comes from respecting people's limits: you need to know when it's okay to push, when you're pushing too hard or too often, and when to concede defeat. If you continue to fight after someone has made up their mind, it can have disastrous effects on a relationship.

And you shouldn't expect to develop that relationship right away, either. Trust is built over time and needs to be earned and re-earned and re-earned again with each new project.

• • •

MATT DRENIK

Creative Director, SOUTH Music and Sound Design;
Recording Artist, El Camino Media, Sony Music
Entertainment

THE BEST THING that you can do as a producer is to get in there and make what you think is the very best piece of work possible. Expectations are always high on every record I've made. Artists have a way they want things to sound. You as a producer have to figure out what will work in the end, and who it will resonate with. You have to make sure the songs match the goals. You can't have a track drenched in reverb or a track where the vocals are buried and expect it to be a number one hit.

There are no rules to the relationship. I'm a positive force. I'm optimistic. I believe that what they're doing can change things for them, whether they're able to quit their job as a bartender and go on the road as a working musician, or whether they can quit touring all the time and become a household name. My job is to be relentless in my pursuit to see they achieve that.

It's about listening and building a level of trust. Any kind of art form needs reassurance, and artists have been pushed to the back of the line their entire lives. When I was in grade school, the kids made fun of me for going to recitals and playing the *Pink Panther* theme. Every artist wants to know that what they're doing is valued. And if they really feel like you're listening and trying to get inside of what they're talking about, they're going to connect with you.

Not every artist is going to want your input. Some will say, "I've written all the songs, they're finished, don't touch them," and at that point you can't do much to help. You have to remember that the artist is in charge, and it's their name on the final piece. You could do as much as you want to help their career: help them write songs, craft their bio, brand identity, help them target markets and audiences . . . but at the end of the day, if the artist isn't into it, there's nothing you can do.

When differences do come up, and they will, I try to highlight the things I like instead of talking about what I don't like. If I hear a song and I love the chorus but I hate the bridge, I'm going to slowly chip away at that bridge over the next few weeks. "Hey, what if we did it like this?" or, "What if we took out that chord?" until eventually it's going to either fall apart or get rewritten.

There's a lot of producers that will push artists to do things they don't want to do because they feel like they know better than the artists. The only reason I don't do that is because I've been on the other side as a recording artist and I remember the feeling. I know how excited they are to be making something from nothing. I know the excitement of that first playback. And I know how badly they want to share their songs with the world.

• • •

BILL WESTBROOK

CEO, No Fences Brand Consulting; former President, Executive Creative Director, Fallon Worldwide

IT'S IMPORTANT NOT to demand, but rather to give the client reasons to agree with your point of view.

ALISON WATSON

Partner, Founder, Legacy House; Owner-President, Four Sisters Productions; former Director, Grind Studios

I DON'T WORK with clients I don't like. I work with friends. When I worked with my clients at Ideo, we ran together. Connecting on something outside of work is huge. You trust people you have a connection with. Especially if you're telling them they have to do something that is going to impact their company. Because it's a friendship, I feel hugely accountable. I would feel bad if I let them down.

BRIAN MILLER

Creative Director, The Walt Disney Company/ Global Marketing

YOU NEED TO build up enough savings in the "trust bank" with clients so you can then, when the time is right, cash in some of the interest. You have to be responsible and responsive to their needs—and show that you're listening and care—so that they listen to you when you want to put the lampshade on your head and dance like a fool.

WHAT THEY SAID, summarized:

- The most important thing is trust.
- Clients need to know you're looking out for their best interests first.
- Listening and reassurance are key.
- Be mindful of how hard you push. Not everyone is going to be receptive to input.
- Figure out how to get clients to agree with your point of view.
- Trust is important.
- A personal connection helps to develop trust, and it makes you feel more accountable to follow through and fulfill your promises.
- The more trust you develop, the more apt clients will be to listen to you.

PUT YOUR CLIENT'S AND COMPANY'S CONCERNS ABOVE YOUR OWN.

And have the ability to discern which are more important.

As makers, we're extremely focused on our projects and achieving our desired goals. Maybe we're looking for the prestige, or affirming accolades. Maybe we want to move up in the organizational pecking order. Or maybe we're just looking to inspire envy among our peers. Never underestimate the motivational power of envy.

As we go from maker to manager, it's important to recalibrate our thinking. Now that we're more connected to clients and tied to their success, and playing bigger roles within our companies, we need to downplay our own self-interests. No client wants a leader who's only driven by winning awards and building their own career. And no company wants to make a long-term investment in a leader who's only in it for themselves. You can still be motivated by awards, career, and envy, but understanding which objectives come first is a must.

• • •

DUNCAN MILNER

Former Global Creative President, Media Arts Lab,
MAL For Good

NOBODY UNDERSTANDS YOUR client's business better than they do. Steve Jobs was my client for many years, and he lived and breathed Apple 24/7. He wanted everything they did to be great. People working on the account went to great lengths to understand his business, but you have to remember your client is living with their problems day in and day out. Creatively, I think separation is a good thing, but you still need to take the time and make the effort to understand their problems so that you can solve them in the best way possible. You may be emotionally invested in your idea in the form it's in now, but that doesn't mean it's solving your client's problem, or that it can't be improved. We need to be honest and unselfish about the things we make and ask, "Is it helping my client, or is it helping me?"

BRIAN MILLER

Creative Director, The Walt Disney Company/
Global Marketing

AS CREATIVES, WE'VE spent years, sometimes decades, being told that our only career currency is cool breakout work. To put that aside is a leap of faith. It's scary. It's being told, "Go ahead, you don't need oxygen. Trust me." And again, it's not mutually exclusive. The best, smartest work is work that is about the core message.

As far as I can tell, there are some people who never suffer one damn bit personally from being selfish about their own needs creatively. There are some who've made lucrative careers doing work that gets noticed at awards shows but doesn't move the sales needle. That's their choice. I prefer the satisfaction of doing work that people love and that also makes clients ask for me again and again.

(Sadly, this business being what it is, I've had to make sure my 401(k) is very robust . . . just in case.)

WHAT THEY SAID, summarized:

- Become as deeply invested in your client's issues as they are.
- Make sure your work is helping your clients and not just you.
- Solving client problems and great creative ideas are not mutually exclusive. Strive for work that does both.
- When clients know you're committed to their success, they'll be more committed to you.

BE MINDFUL OF
THE PERSON ABOVE
THE PERSON ABOVE.

To know what's really driving decisions and tastes, you need to look beyond your direct contacts at the entire chain of command. That means understanding your client's boss, and, within your own organization, your boss's boss. What are *their* concerns? What are the pressures they're facing? What are their likes and dislikes? What are their land mines? And what are their relationships and expectations with the people you report in to? Understanding their agendas, the mechanics of their relationships, and their success metrics will help you, help them, and help everyone in between.

This isn't about going over anyone's head. But the more perspectives you get, the more complete your understanding, and the better informed your creative work will be—which will make all of those people that you look up at look up to you in appreciation.

• •

KRISTEN GROVE MØLLER

Creative Director, 72andSunny

OUR JOB IS to help our direct clients look good and succeed at *their* job, which means helping them look awesome in front of their bosses.

Often, they're representing your work as they present it further up the chain of command. This happens a lot with Google, one of my clients, where there are many layers but ultimately one decisionmaker. You want your client to be able to represent the work as well as you could, so that means giving them all of the ammunition and coaching they need to sell it and making sure their own presentation is bulletproof.

As strong as our relationship may be with our day-to-day clients, we have to think about the layers above them when it comes to feedback: what they expect on a project and what their overall concerns are. When it comes to feedback, you need to filter through it to understand what that person's boss (or bosses) actually wants. When you have several layers of communication, there's always the danger of misinterpretation. It's like the game of telephone, when you're speaking into one person's ear and that person speaks in to another person and it continues and ultimately the thing that is said is totally different than what was first spoken. Since you don't always get the exact information, ask as many questions as possible, even dumb questions, because the more you know, the more precise you can be with your solutions.

It's also good to know where each piece of feedback is coming from, so that you know how heavily to weigh it, to determine if someone is overreacting to what was said and asking for more changes than are really necessary. I don't know how many times I've been in a meeting with a higher-up who says, "That wasn't what I meant." Then when you hear what they did want, you're like, "Oh, okay, I get it," but you've wasted a month and it's a total reset. You want to get straight to the person who matters the most, but if you can't, it's important to interpret feedback as best you can and know what to listen to.

The more you can keep your client's bosses (and your own bosses) in the loop so there are no big surprises for them down the line, the better. Working in a vacuum is dangerous. Let them into the kitchen versus trying to build up tension or surprising people with the final meal. Try to avoid preparing the meal before you know if anyone has any allergies.

WHAT THEY SAID, summarized:

- It's important to make your clients look good and succeed at their job.
- Be mindful that in many instances the people you present to are not the end of the chain of command.
- Extrapolate what is being said by whom. Determine what the top leaders are saying and answer their concerns.
- The best way to avoid surprises is to share more, and share more often, with the people who matter most.

MANAGING CLIENTS & HIGHER-UPS

DON'T RISE SO HIGH THAT YOU LOSE SIGHT OF THE PEOPLE BELOW YOU

DON'T RISE SO HIGH THAT YOU LOSE SIGHT OF THE PEOPLE BELOW YOU.

Assuming that you're not running a company or near the very top of one, you probably have to manage relationships with people both above and below you. Those above that are running things, and those below that are making things. It's a tough position to be in. Yes, it's important to stay connected to your higher-ups. After all, they're going to teach you things, they know everything there is to know about the company, and most importantly, they hand out the raises and promotions. But as you get chummy with the folks above, don't lose sight of those below. They're the ones who make you look good, and are intrinsic to your day-to-day success. If they sense that you're climbing your way up the ladder while forgetting all the people who are helping you get there, they may begin to resent you, alienate you from the group, or even report you to those people at the top.

You need to become adept at managing up as well as managing down. Build strong relationships with your managers and leaders while still cultivating meaningful, trusting relationships with the people that work for you. Your career is dependent on building relationships in both directions. Be sure to ascend carefully. It's a long way to fall.

• • •

VALERIE VAN GALDER

CEO, Depressed Cake Shop; Producer,
former President of Marketing, Sony Pictures

MY DAD REALLY took management, and what he learned in business school, seriously. One of the things I very much absorbed from him was the way he manages teams. He owned a chain of Midas muffler shops, and the way that he managed his employees who were car mechanics was a master class in loyalty. They loved working for my dad because he incentivized them and he treated them well, to the point that if one of their children was sick, he took care of them. There was no end to his loyalty. He taught us that everyone, no matter the job, requires the same amount of respect as everyone else. So, for me, it always became, "Be protective of your team, invest them in the success, never undercut or undermine them, and they will do good work for you."

JEFF GILES

Executive Editor, *Vanity Fair*;
Author, *The Edge of Everything*

THE PUBLISHING WORLD is always in such jeopardy that the tension is unbelievably high and morale is incredibly precarious. It gets more and more important to empathize with people, yet we have more and more pressure to get the job done with fewer resources and less gratitude. I've worked in places where the people working for you end up getting hurt all the time.

I've never been that worried about the leaders who have all the information, these great lives, and much more of the money. But in previous jobs, I've definitely worried about the people beneath me who weren't always told the truth by management, and who were continually scared for their futures. The hardest thing about being a middle manager is being a firewall between the folks at the top who run things and the staff, where you're like, "Don't worry about it. I've got you." I can't say I always succeeded at it, but I've tried. You need to focus on your people and help them feel secure.

Newsweek could be a very corporate place, but if someone in the company was in trouble or their house burned down, they were fantastic in a crisis. When a longtime senior editor passed away, they had a service for him. He wasn't a top editor, but many people knew him and he left behind a wife and family. After the service concluded, Katharine Graham went up to his son, who was eighteen, and asked, "You're going to college, aren't you?" The son replied *yes*, to which Katharine said, "Good. I'll pay for it." That always really struck me. In this modern era of downsizing and corporate pressures, where empathy goes out the window and you stop thinking of people as people, she showed immense and unrequired compassion.

ROB SCHWARTZ

Chief Executive Officer at TBWA\CHIAT\DAY, New York

JAY CHIAT, FOUNDER and former president of Chiat\Day, didn't have an office. He sat in the middle of the agency. He wasn't the king of the castle; he was a battlefield general who wanted to be situated among all his people. There was no obvious delineation of who was above and who was below. It was just about "us."

I'm reminded of something Confucius said: "If they work for me, then I work for them." It's very much the basis of leadership today, and the way I like to work. I want to know what I can do with the people who work for me, together, to make the collective great.

I've never felt like I'm above anyone else in this business. I take the subway to work every day. I walk the halls and stay connected to as many people as I can. I stay connected to their work and make sure I'm in it with them. I don't want to lose touch with what's getting made, and the people making it.

BRIAN MILLER

Creative Director, The Walt Disney Company/Global Marketing

I'VE SEEN PEOPLE'S mindfulness of their superiors go way too far into shallow obsequiousness and even neglect of the needs and concerns of everyone beneath them. I lead not in a supply-side way, but by making sure those underneath me in the chain of command (who are counting on me to lead) are happy, engaged, encouraged, nourished, and taken care of.

TED PRICE

President and Founder, Insomniac Games

WE HAVE MULTIPLE large projects in production at any time, so it's really easy for creative teams to feel like they're not getting the full story on what's happening, or the *why* behind the decisions that are being made. At Insomniac, we make a big effort to pull back the curtains every single day.

As an example, every day I share an "ask me anything" email with the whole company. In those emails I or someone else in leadership is answering a question that's come from someone on the team. Team members don't hold back, and the questions that I get asked are often pretty challenging. I think our constant push for transparency puts us all on a level playing field where Insomniacs feel more comfortable asking tough questions. It also forces us to address problems early—before they become raging fires.

• • •

WHAT THEY SAID, summarized:

- Invest in your team.
- Do right by your team and they will do right by you.
- Leaders have the information and power. Use your understanding to help your team feel more secure.
- Stay connected and situated with your team.
- Take a servant leadership approach in the way you care for those you lead.
- Transparency and constant communication helps eliminate a *them vs. us* environment.

everyone AT THE TABLE DESERVES RESPECT

(even if it's not apparent why yet)

EVERYONE AT THE TABLE DESERVES
RESPECT

(even if it's not apparent why yet).

t's easy to dismiss the people in the room who aren't the main decisionmakers. After all, their opinions, for better or worse, don't have as much bearing as some of the other, more influential, folks. However, while their comments might be less informed, their demeanors less assured, or their titles significantly smaller, it would be a mistake to ignore them.

No one knows what the future may bring. The smallest voice today might be the biggest voice tomorrow. That meek junior-level person at the end of the table who routinely gets ignored might one day take over the role of lead client or supervisor . . . and will probably be plotting their revenge. Or they may end up heading someplace else and taking over the lead role there, and what could have been an incredible new business opportunity for you now becomes a nonstarter. Or they may be the most involved on your project day-to-day. While they may not be the most important in the room, they may be the most hands on, and the person you want most invested in your project moving forward.

Respect shouldn't just be reserved for the folks at the head of the table who hold the gavel. Nor should it be solely reserved for everyone on the client side. It's something that needs to be given to all members of your team. Have the foresight to acknowledge everyone at the table, and when the people at the head inevitably change, you'll have a better chance of keeping your own seat.

ROB SCHWARTZ

Chief Executive Officer at TBWA\CHIAT\DAY, New York

THERE'S A TECHNIQUE that many big companies employ where they invite several layers of management to meetings, from the CMO, to the next-in-line CMO, all the way down to the most junior person. When you're making your pitch to sell creative ideas, if you're just playing to the CMO, and only making eye contact or conversation with the CMO, you're going to be in trouble, because all of those other people are going to be involved and empowered to make decisions. And if you're alienating them, those decisions may not be in your favor. And boy will you be sorry.

You also have to be careful because those people are eventually going to move up the ladder. Years ago, we pitched a brave idea to one of our clients. He rejected it, and after the meeting (then-CCO) Lee Clow turned to me and said, "You know who that client was? He was the guy who used to get coffee for us when we did the good stuff." I remember very distinctly thinking, "Be nice to the people on the way up, because they may be around when you're on top."

MARGARET KEENE

Executive Creative Director, Mullen LA

THE PERSON YOU disregard, intentionally or not, becomes your most senior client in ten years. Guaranteed. But more importantly, huge ideas can often come from the people farthest away from the rules and the politics of the brand. When they feel like their input is welcome, they're people you can get really great information and feedback from.

Note about young, shy, or introverted creative people: there are some who will bury them or overlook what they have to say in meetings. Spend extra time pulling them out of their shells. Help them articulate their thoughts and find the tools and the strength to stand up for their work. And push your young women to take charge of their ideas and lean on you when they need support. I've seen many of them get talked down to, talked over, or completely disregarded even when they are strong and persuasive. Often, only a senior leader can remedy the situation.

BRIAN MILLER

Creative Director, The Walt Disney Company/ Global Marketing

MORE THAN JUST treating clients and others as "allies for the future," this kind of respect leads to better work in the immediate term. When you listen to everyone in the room, you build allies for the very work you're trying to sell. Oh, and if you pull your head out of your ass, you just may learn something— those people sit with their company's needs all day, every day. They know way more than you do.

WHAT THEY SAID, summarized:

- Don't alienate anyone in a meeting, regardless of their level.
- The way you treat someone today could have a detrimental effect later.
- Great ideas can come from anyone. Don't overlook or disregard someone who is young, shy, or introverted.
- Being respectful of everyone can help build allies.
- The less powerful people in the room are often more involved day-to-day. It's good to have their buy-in on projects.

PUT A RING
ON IT.

When you say "I do" to the job of creative leader, you're entering into a committed relationship with both clients and the company you work for. You're no longer just an occasional visitor to meetings, ducking your head in to present your work and then leaving once the higher-level discussions begin. You're not just an on-again, off-again contributor and contact. You're entering into a deeper, longer-term relationship and becoming a consistent, trusted voice in the room. And that requires taking certain vows.

Learn as much as you can about your client's business and the overall industry landscape. You're someone who is important to their broader business goals, so study the competition and keep up with the industry trends. Make their enemies your enemies. Make their concerns your concerns. Invest yourself in their success. Find out what their pain points are and what keeps them up late at night. And, finally, become familiar with the entire chain of command, so you can find out how your client's success is being measured and how you can help them reach their goals.

The same goes for committing to your company. Figure out their concerns. Identify their strengths and vulnerabilities and become invested in their success, as well. When you show them love and care, they'll be supportive of you, too. Until a new job do you part.

• • •

ALISON WATSON

Partner, Founder, Legacy House; Owner-President, Four Sisters Productions; former Director, Grind Studios

CLIENTS WANT TO know that this is more than just a gig for you. They need to know someone else gives a shit. They want candor and genuine passion, not bullshit. When the client can see you're in it for them, it gives you the unique privilege to be open, honest, and direct.

One of the companies I consult with specializes in wellness programs. I had to tell them that they needed to shut down twelve of their programs because they didn't fit into their brand. These are a huge source of pride for them. Much of how they react is going to be based on the source, and since they know I have their best interests in mind, I have permission to tell them these things.

I'm dealing with people at the C-suite level of Fortune 500 companies. I don't pretend to know everything. I don't pretend to be an equal. And I don't hide the fact that I come from a creative world and not their own. But because I'm direct and don't bullshit people, and because I'm confident enough to admit I don't know everything (I tend to say things like, "I can't promise you I'm not wrong, but pretty sure I'm not"), and because I become deeply invested, educated, and passionate about their company's success, they listen.

SHANNON WASHINGTON

Group Executive Creative Director, R/GA

MY TEAM WOULD get these five-hundred-word stream-of-consciousness feedback emails from our client, and because I knew her, knew her personality, and connected with her personally, I could usually discern what she was saying. I'd just send a short note back saying, "So do this?" and she'd be like, "Yeah."

I knew my client was dealing with low-performing ads that had to work harder. I knew what she was up against. There was a sense of partnership, and that I was invested in her success, which was important. And the enemy was the same for us: How do we surpass expectations and become relevant? It was a joint goal. And by making her and her team feel like they were part of the process, I could see in real time what her intake process was and get reactions before they became conclusions.

When we would challenge each other, it was done through a lens of respect because we both believed in what we were saying. There was a common connection there: "I feel you. I'm not agreeing with you, but I feel you."

When a client doesn't like working with you, you have to recognize that they're not vibing and let someone else get involved. I've had to say, "This person isn't going to respond well to me presenting the work. I think we need someone else to do it." I realize the greater good is the business and the work. I won't get in the way of that.

WHAT THEY SAID, summarized:

- Clients want to see that you care.
- When a client sees you're in it for them, they'll open up and be willing to listen.
- Be direct. Don't bullshit people.
- Having a special connection with a client makes you more indispensable.
- Having common goals strengthens the connection.
- Recognize when a client doesn't want to work with you and have the presence to let someone else take the lead.

ASPIRE TO BE A CLIENT WHISPERER

ASPIRE TO BE A CLIENT WHISPERER.

A "whisperer" is a person with the unique ability to connect with someone or something on a deeper level than anyone else. You've heard it applied to dogs, horses, babies, and—thanks to Jennifer Love Hewitt—ghosts.

Client whisperers have the unique ability to communicate with a client in ways that others can't. They're a calming force when things are tense and can talk a client off a ledge. They're able to sway a client one way or the other. And when there's a big decision to make, they're the sought-after voice of reason that clients want to hear.

There are several ways to become a client whisperer. It starts with earning their trust, and demonstrating that you're coming from a place of sincerity. It comes from hearing what they have to say versus pushing your own agenda. It comes from having a keen understanding of their business, a signal that you're just as invested and knowledgeable as they are and are therefore a credible source. And it comes from being able to interpret what they mean but can't always put into words. A client whisperer is generally able to decipher feedback in ways no one else can.

If you can become a client whisperer, you become a valuable commodity and someone who's extremely hard to replace. Your client is going to demand you stay on their business, and your company is going to be hard-pressed to let you go. Do whatever you can to build a special connection with your client.

And, if it's at all possible, ghosts, too.

DUNCAN MILNER

Former Global Creative President, Media Arts Lab, MAL For Good

AT THE END of the day, you're always trying to solve the client's problem. If they feel you're not solving their problem, it's a very short-term win to sell them on an idea that ends up not being effective. Tom McElligott, who I worked with at Chiat in Toronto, once said, "Clients don't buy ads, they buy a relationship." If clients trust you, they're more inclined to buy good work from you.

I remember the time it clicked for me. I'd sent Steve Jobs some layouts for outdoor boards for the colored clamshell Apple iBook. It was a bunch of kids and different people lying down interacting with the product. And I remember he called me at home on a Friday night to talk about them. I was trying to sell him on how good the photography was, and he said to me, "Duncan, they're just not great, and Apple deserves great." I didn't actually believe that they were great, I was just telling him they were great, to get them approved and move on, and in that moment I realized that furthering my agenda wasn't going to get me very far, or earn the trust of my client. If I was going to win Steve's trust, I had to always look at everything through the prism of, "Is this the best thing for Apple?"

Steve really demanded honesty and integrity. When he asked you what you thought of the work you were presenting, he didn't just want you to sell the work to him. He wanted your honest opinion, and for you to tell him if it really was great or not. That trust he had in us, who he perceived as experts in our field, was paramount.

Steve surrounded himself with people that he believed in and people that he trusted. It was a very small circle. When Lee Clow (former CCO, Chiat\Day) brought me down to work on Apple, it took a while for Steve to trust me. I was just the guy who sat to the left of Lee. But over time he started to develop a trust and reassurance, to the point where he would say, "Lee, what do you think? Duncan, what do you think?" When he believed you wanted to do the right thing for Apple, he listened. And he reconsidered his own opinions if yours called for it.

Years later, after Steve's passing, Phil Schiller, SVP of worldwide advertising, became our head client on Apple. He'd spent all those years in the room with us when we were presenting things to Steve, and so there was that same trust. When he was moving on to run the App Store business, he told us, "You guys never understood that you had this super power. All you ever had to do to convince me to buy something was to tell me that you believe I should do this and it's the right thing to do." And, of course, I remember going, "Really, it could have been that easy?!"

• • •

SAM OLIVER

Group Creative Director, Apple

I WAS NEVER one who loved new business. Some people have that knack for being great in that first meeting, and being able to dazzle a room. That was never me. I quite like the adrenaline rush of getting the work together and coming up with ideas quickly, but I didn't like having to sell to someone—or sell myself to someone that I don't know. I much prefer having an intimate, trusting relationship already and we can just talk about the work, and talk about it in an honest way. In new business they're evaluating you on two things. Do I want to work with this person, and do I like the work? When it's a client that you know, it's just about the work. It's a privileged position to talk to someone, whether it's a boss or a client, about the work without having to prove yourself or earn trust as an employee or a vendor. I think you get to a better place that way.

— WHAT THEY SAID, summarized: —

- Becoming a client whisperer takes time.
- If clients trust you, they're more likely to buy good work from you.
- You're more likely to become a whisperer if clients see you're honest and trustworthy.
- Being a whisperer is a privileged position.
- A whisperer relationship can make the work better.

DON'T TREAT INSIGHTS OR IDEAS LIKE BURIED TREASURE

DON'T TREAT
INSIGHTS OR IDEAS
LIKE BURIED TREASURE.

'll get straight to the point. Just get to the point. When you're presenting, don't waste time teasing your work with long preambles or a lengthy list of caveats or by sharing drawn-out personal stories. And definitely, definitely, *definitely* don't start with, "Like so-and-so just said" and then repeat what so-and-so just said, which everyone in the room has already heard, which no one wants to hear again.

Senior executives haven't got the time or patience for long lead-ups to the things they came to see. And, generally speaking, they can see through any bullshit. It's important to read the room, understand the body language, and gauge the overall vibe. How has the meeting gone thus far, and, based on that, are people going to be receptive to what you're showing? Are the people you're presenting to in a good headspace? Are they asking, "How long is this going to take?" Are they looking at their phones? Are their arms crossed? You need to know when there's a gale force wind in your face and when you need to condense or eliminate your preamble altogether. Or when you should just say, "You know what, we can do this some other time," and not show the work at all.

Get to the good stuff fast, not last. You might be surprised by their ability to get it without explaining every dirty detail. When you learn to read a room and connect with your audience, the process of selling things gets a whole lot easier.

SEEMA MILLER

Cofounder, President, WolfGang

IN SCHOOL, SHAKESPEARE taught me that "brevity is the soul of wit." In college, my journalism teacher told me "don't bury the lede." Then, in advertising, I saw three-minute setups for a thirty-second script. The irony was apparent to everyone except the creative delivering it in earnest. Spike Lee distilled a two-hour film down to six words in order to pitch it: "Black man infiltrates Ku Klux Klan." Eliminate everything superfluous until the defining idea shines in relief.

SAM OLIVER

Group Creative Director, Apple

I GET IMPATIENT when people ramble around and don't get to the point quickly or say things simply. I love the fact that Steve Jobs banned PowerPoint presentations. He thought that if it was a good idea it could be said without having to look at three hundred slides. It was quite ruthless but it was necessary to keep things simple. What I've noticed since going client side at Apple is we're extremely direct. We have a few setup slides with our strategy and intentions. They're short, uncomplicated, and not attempts to try to prove ourselves or be overly clever. And look, since being simple is a challenge, I'm always impressed when people can.

SURESH NAIR

Global Chief Strategy Officer, Grey Worldwide

I LEARNED A lot from our former Chief Creative Officer Tor Myhren, who used to say, "Start with the idea and go from there." Until then, the agency mantra was this big song and dance in the strategy section, the creative section, and then the Chief Creative Officer does a setup, and the head creative on the project does a setup. It feels so dated now, but it still happens. We used to call it "the rain delay" because it delayed the start of the meeting.

TED PRICE

President and Founder, Insomniac Games

WE PLACE A great emphasis on strong presentations. That's because, as we've grown, success has been dependent on getting buy-in from our own teams on concepts, pitching our games to external partners, and then convincing our fans that what we're making is worthwhile.

We've spent a lot of time trying to improve our presentation approach. Brevity, impact, responsiveness, polish—there's a giant list of essential ingredients we believe are important for any effective presentation. And I'm not talking necessarily about a full game pitch or a marketing campaign. It could be a new feature, a story change, a weapon design . . . but selling the idea is key. Plus, we absolutely recognize that we're a mélange of personalities and everyone's style is different. So, for us, we're constantly tweaking what "great presentation" actually means.

WHAT THEY SAID, summarized:

- Get to the point (unless you've got something smart or insightful to say).
- Don't bury the lede or overshadow a good idea with a long, complicated setup.
- Try leading with the big idea rather than going through lengthy preambles.
- Don't try to prove yourself or be overly clever with a lengthy lead-up.
- Being simple and direct can be challenging.
- You can live or die on how you present work.

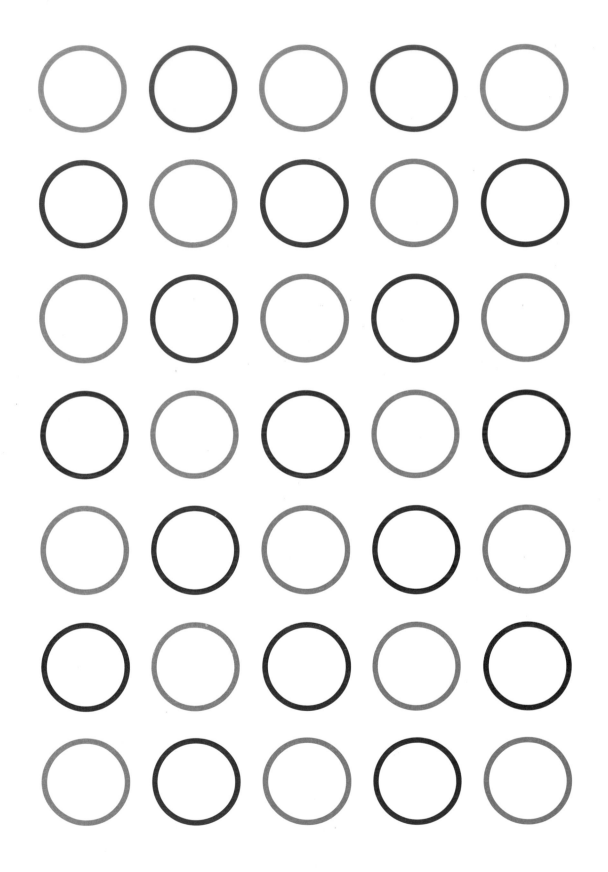

THE WORK

SECTION 4
THE WORK

Things just got super complicated. Instead of birthing great ideas, you've become something more akin to a doula, encouraging new parents to push harder and take deep breaths. For some, it's sweet relief from the pressure, continual disappointment, and weekend-swallowing slog, but for many, this absence of creative fulfillment leaves them with cavernous voids and feelings of insecurity that often manifest themselves in not-so-healthy ways.

While we may have pushed hard for our favorite ideas in the past and allowed our creative zeal to guide our decisionmaking, our new leadership positions come with greater responsibility and accountability. How and why we push for things needs to be carefully considered. As Rachel Shukert, executive producer of *The Baby-Sitters Club* and co-executive producer of *GLOW,* puts it, "Some people don't know how to get the best out of other people, and only know being the savior and doing it themselves." Adds Sam Bergen, Chief Creative Officer at Beats by Dre, "When you're a leader, this is your team. This is a job. It isn't a cycle that gets refreshed."

One of the biggest issues for me when I first took a leadership role was knowing when to send teams back to make revisions to work, and when to suggest or make the changes myself. I was so consumed with doing great work and getting things perfect (for my client at the time, Apple, anything less than perfect was considered an atrocity against humankind) that I sometimes wrestled projects away from people prematurely, without giving them the chance to figure things out for themselves, which impeded their personal growth and skill development.

I also had to learn how to balance my deepening client engagement with my own deep creative conviction. While it was absolutely imperative I earn my client's trust and make sure they knew I had their best interests in mind, I still needed the freedom to be able to disagree with them, to push them out of their comfort zones, and to fight for work I believed in. It's a precarious position to be in. I've had clients who have spoken candidly to my supervisors and asked that I not push so hard, while others have expressed that they appreciate my passion and wish others on the team were equally zealous. Over the years, I've learned the importance of knowing the personalities involved, and weighing risk and reward.

We need to look at the broader impact of our work and take a more holistic approach to selling it. What are the risks of pushing teams and clients too hard, or not pushing hard enough? How involved do we get in the work in our elevated positions? What are the consequences of failure, and how can we reduce the risks of our work missing the mark? This section offers several strategies for how to approach the work in our leadership roles in ways that lead to lasting relationships, higher job satisfaction, and overall success.

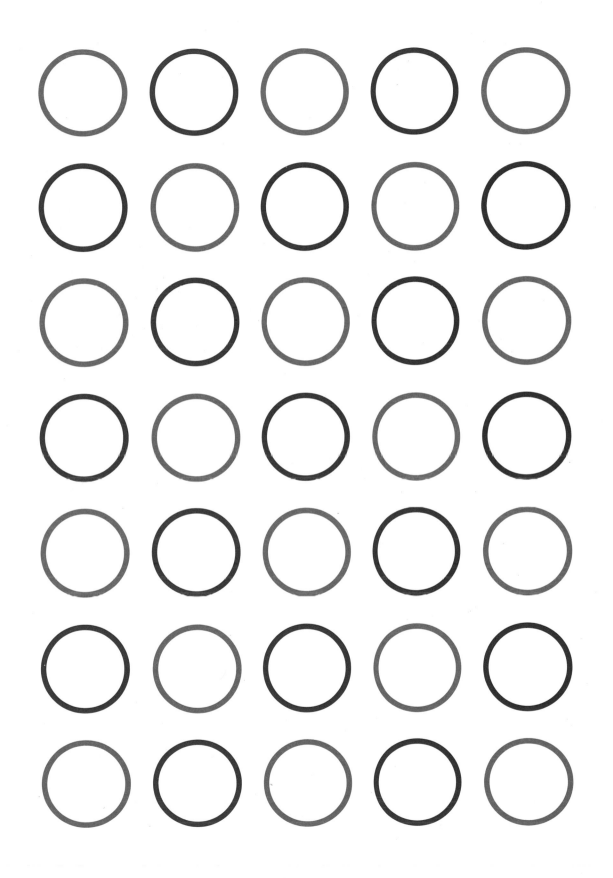

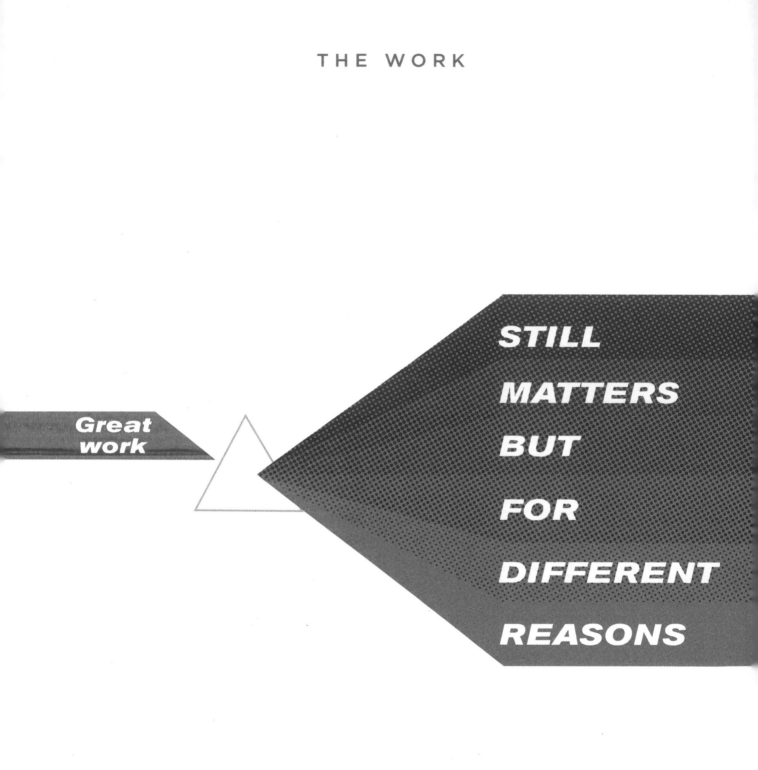

Great work

STILL MATTERS BUT FOR DIFFERENT REASONS

GREAT WORK
STILL MATTERS, BUT FOR DIFFERENT REASONS.

Your work is your resume. Thus, the quality of the work you make is a hugely important facet of your job. In fact, it probably largely contributed to your promotion to creative leader. When you make great things, it can lead to awards, acclaim, a higher salary, oohs and ahhs from frenemies in the industry, a sweeter job, and ultimately it can lengthen your creative career—which, if you're like me, you worry about your expiration date way too much.

But even with all of the new benefits, managers need to understand that their work has broader objectives beyond being their personal industry calling card. Great work helps bring in new business, something your company relies on to keep its doors open. It attracts new creative talent, something that you rely on as a leader to make great work (and also keeps the doors open). And when your company is making great things and being talked about, it improves company morale, which keeps talented people from looking around for new gigs (and, yes, keeps the doors open). Most importantly, great work helps your clients reach their objectives and keep their jobs, and that helps you keep your job.

· · ·

DAVID ANGELO

Founder, Chairman, David & Goliath;
Founder, Today I'm Brave

IN GENERAL, TODAY'S creative leader needs to redefine what great work means. It isn't just something that fills your shelves with awards or feeds your ego. It's much bigger than that. Today, great work must go beyond the trend of one-off stunts. It needs to go beyond being just the envy of our peers. Great work needs to have lasting impact that can inspire a mindset for social change. In order for that to happen, today's creative leader needs to adopt a more big-picture mentality: from the type of work they create, to the effect that work will have on the world around them. When you do that, you won't just be seen as an ad-maker, but a change-maker.

RON RADZINER

President, Design Partner, Marmol Radziner Architects

ALMOST EVERY DESIGNER in our office is working on multiple projects at once. All of your attention isn't focused on a single project, so it helps us not take a particular project too personally. And we can all be open to each other's creative input to work together toward the strongest architecture of each project.

• • •

RICK COLBY

Former President, Executive Creative Director,
Colby & Partners Dentsu

WHEN YOU'RE A copywriter or art director your main focus, your primary motivation, is to get something good for your portfolio. Which makes sense because you're trying to get yourself noticed, trying to maintain a career and prove to everyone, including yourself, that you've got talent. But when you're more senior, the work takes on an added level of importance. It becomes more of a means to an end instead of just being the end. The work becomes a way to build business and attract new business. By doing work that gets noticed, makes clients happy, makes for case studies, and yes, that even wins awards, you're showing that your work isn't just creative, it's effective.

Every time we set out to do a campaign, our primary goal was to solve a problem for our clients. If that doesn't work, it fails everybody, including us. We might have great creative work to show, but if there's no success story to attach to it, it's completely toothless for new business purposes. Not to mention the client it was for is probably disappointed.

After California Pizza Kitchen came to us asking us how to increase traffic in their restaurants, we created a billboard campaign around several of their menu items. The billboards were contextualized, so a board for garlic chicken pizza went above a dentist office, and a board for the BBQ chicken pizza went over a cleaners. While they got a lot of attention for being creative, it was because of their success and the thinking behind them that we were able to use their case study in new business meetings. And case studies like that one were one of the big reasons why we continually made the finals for pitches against agencies that were much bigger than us.

WHAT THEY SAID, summarized:

- Great work needs to have lasting impact.
- Today's creative people need to be thinking big picture.
- Your distance from the work allows you to think about it differently than its creators.
- As a leader, the effectiveness of the work takes on added importance.
- Work becomes even stronger and more marketable when it has a success story attached to it.

THE WORK

A

POV

IS

IMP

A POV IS
IMP.

Your job is pretty simple when you think about it: have a perspective on creative work, and be able to say things like, "I like this," or, "I think this could be better" with conviction. Most importantly, you need to be able to understand and communicate why creative ideas work or why they don't and, in the case of the latter, what can be done to improve them.

Your team is relying on you to be direct, clear, and decisive. They want to know that when they walk away from a meeting with you, they understand exactly what they need to work on. They also want to know that if you have to present their work to clients or others in your company, you'll represent it with equal conviction and share the same viewpoint. If you typically wilt like a flower in the summer heat, they'll lose faith in you as their leader.

Having a point of view comes with the higher title and salary. You need to have one to do your job. But keep in mind that your creative instincts need to be right more often than not; otherwise, you become an impediment to those working below you and a liability to the company and client you work for. And, worst-case scenario, your team bypasses you and presents it to the people above you, or the client asks for someone else to work on their business.

Okay, so maybe your job isn't so simple, after all.

TARAS WAYNER

Chief Creative Officer, Saatchi & Saatchi

ONE OF THE biggest mistakes many of us make when we make the leap from creative to manager is that we go into the job without a vision. That lack of vision leads to new creative directors getting stuck in something I call "the drift": we arrive with the burning desire to do "great work" and make our mark. But we often arrive with no vision for what constitutes great work, or how to direct work to become great, and no filters by which to judge "great work." So, we drift our way through it. We make statements like, "I'll know it when I see it," or, "It's just not good enough." This eventually leads to frustration from the creatives, the strategists, and the account team, as well as the newly minted creative director. These actions lead to a demotivated team guessing what their boss wants.

The best thing a new CD can do to avoid the drift is to have a vision.

What the best creative leaders like Susan Hoffman, Gerry Graf, and Nick Law all have in common is that they helped craft the great work they're known for by having a vision for how to get to that great work. Even though each of their styles of work is different, their vision gave them the tools and lenses to properly judge work and nurture it to greatness. And, when they killed work, they used the principles of their vision to give a reason for why it wasn't right, along with direction for how to get to that great work again.

The best CDs I've worked for didn't just do great work, they understood *why* the work was great. They had a strong belief for why they didn't like something, or why they did. The best agencies I've worked for had a shared vision. Creative, business leads operations, and finance all aligned behind the same vision. The opposite is also true. The worst jobs I had were working for people without a vision, and for companies whose leaders didn't share in the same vision. Understanding this has helped me make the right job choices and grow into a more confident creative director.

So, state an intention and find a vision and then go out there and do great work.

MATT DRENIK

Creative Director, SOUTH Music and Sound Design;
Recording Artist, El Camino Media, Sony Music Entertainment

I THINK IT'S your job to have a firm point of view on whether the band you're working with has anything to say. This is where your experience comes in. I've dealt with many garage rock bands and psychedelic rock bands and stoner rock bands and hip-hop bands and you start to categorize them, subconsciously. And so you're like, "Is this any good? Does this hold up to other records? Can you put a Petty song on and then put this song on and does it hang in there? Or is it just a dud?" And so you have to make decisions based on those questions, and try to make that record better as you're recording.

SUSAN HOFFMAN

Chairman, Wieden & Kennedy

DAN WIEDEN AND David Kennedy were amazing bosses. They didn't meddle in the work. They didn't allow their own styles to dictate everyone else's. They allowed everyone to have a voice. When Janet, Kristy, and I presented the Nike "Revolution" spot, Dan and David looked at us and said, "Are you kidding? We can't use a Beatles song." And in the afternoon they called us back in and said, "You know, that's the only thing that excited us. Let's present it."

They were clear on what appealed to them emotionally and they challenged us, but with their gut and intuition. One time my creative director partner and I fought extremely hard to present a campaign to a client that Dan felt was not right for them. We argued and asked Dan, "Since when were creative directors not allowed to present work they believed in?" He said, "Fine, if you feel that strongly, present it, but I'm just giving you a warning." So we presented it to the client and the client yelled at us and said, "Why the hell would we buy this?" It was a brutal meeting. And when we came home, Dan didn't say, "I told you so." He said, "Well, you felt strongly about it so now you know." He let us make mistakes. One of the sayings here is "Fail Harder." That was a fail harder moment.

DAVID OYELOWO

Actor, *Selma*; Producer, *Come Away*;
Director, *The Water Man*

A VISION IS absolutely imperative for success. But it's on you as a leader to be confident enough to be able to say "I actually don't know." What happens is this allows the person working for you to step in and say, "I think I know what you need." Or, "I think I know someone or some way to get you what you want." Being able to say I don't know is still leadership, and I think people respect that.

JOE RUSSO

Executive Producer, *Community*; Director,
Avengers: Endgame; Founder, Bullitt Productions

OUR SUCCESS COMES from being collaborative in all endeavors and working with other creative artists from the inception of a story. We work as a team to look for a bantering of thoughts and ideas that propel a concept forward. We are very thoughtful and map out detailed outlines so that when we are communicating our vision for a project we are able to be clear. We find that this clarity and cohesive view allows everyone to be involved in the picture.

• • •

WHAT THEY SAID, summarized:

- Have a vision and be specific with your intentions and direction.
- A vision gives you a lens to properly evaluate work and know what is great.
- It's important to surround yourself with people who are aligned with your vision.
- Your job is to have a strong point of view, and to improve things when possible.
- When people feel strongly about something, give them the opportunity to fail.
- Its okay to sometimes say, "I don't know."
- Sharing your vision with everyone encourages collaboration and involvement.

Fingerprints can leave smudges

FINGERPRINTS
CAN LEAVE SMUDGES.

Every creative person is familiar with that leader who, due either to their own insecurity or an unresolved desire to make things, needlessly tweaks the work, or worse, adds their ideas into the mix (bonus points if they recommended their own ideas to the client). We all know this creative leader. And we all hate working for them.

It's not an easy thing to go from being the source of creative ideas to their supervisor. However, it's essential for creative leaders to let the makers do the making and to refrain from asking for gratuitous revisions or additions. There is nothing more frustrating than a fussy boss who is still trying to prove their creative worth by altering the work. And no one wants to compete with a boss who, by nature of their title alone, has an obvious advantage in selling their own work over their team's. It often comes across as a lack of confidence in your team's abilities. After all, if you don't trust them enough to do the work themselves, then they must be doing something wrong . . . right?

This type of leadership is all sorts of unhealthy for a creative group. It affects morale, job performance, and will likely shorten tenures. Yes, there are going to be times when creative leaders do need to weigh in, make changes to the work, or even lob in their own idea . . . and recommend it. But this should be the exception, not the norm. Otherwise it becomes destructive.

Try being a conductor versus trying to play every instrument in the band. Whenever possible, let your creative people search for answers and unearth the ideas themselves. They'll feel more ownership and pride in the process and will continue to develop the skills that will make them great at their jobs. Plus, your relationship to them will be a *lot* less messy.

• •

BARRY WEISS

Founder, President, RECORDS; former CEO, RCA/Jive Records; former Chairman, UMG East Coast Labels

IF YOU CAN'T watch someone else being creative and can't get comfortable with your role as an executive, then you shouldn't make the switch. You're just going to torture yourself. Sometimes it's a growing process where a creative slowly evolves into that executive, rather than go cold turkey. It's over a period of time where maybe they realized, "I'm a good producer but not a great producer," or maybe, "I'm a competent songwriter but not an amazing songwriter, but boy am I an amazing A&R person." From what I've seen, some of the best baseball managers weren't the superstar players or gifted athletes, but they were the journeymen players. They saw the ups and the downs of toiling in the minors and so they had more empathy and understanding of the people playing for them.

There are a lot of record producers, writers, or artists who want to migrate and become executives. But a lot of times when

people try to do both, it gets really murky and really challenging. If that artist can't play their position, it just doesn't work. If you look at the annals of the record business, there are a lot of failed joint ventures where the artist blows up, becomes a magnet for talent for the label, and then can't transition from being an artist to being a businessperson. They stifle the other artists and that's that.

The challenge that you always have is that there's only room for one artist in the studio, and you don't want the artist to think that the A&R person is guiding the creative process with them. Artists by definition are narcissists, and they don't want to feel challenged. They want that person pushing them to make a great record, but not competing with them and honing in on their creative process. It's a fine line.

If you look at Jimmy and LA Reid, who were incredible record producers, when they became executives they stopped being producers. It was really a turning point where they made the switch and didn't try to keep producing the hits, too. I think they were able to get their creative "jones" by being a part of the process but not being the whole process and just playing their A&R role. They didn't need to sit behind the console in the recording studio and turn knobs like they were in their former lives. I always look at that and say that's the best way to do it: when you stop cold turkey being a pure creative and become a record executive.

ANGUS WALL

Producer, *13th*; Editor, *The Girl with the Dragon Tattoo*, *The Social Network*; Founder, Rock Paper Scissors Editorial, A52, Elastic

I'M ACTUALLY SURPRISED that I don't miss individual achievement more. But I don't. Seeing other people being successful is more important than my own success. I get deep satisfaction out of that. I really mean that. Truthfully. And maybe I'm just getting older.

It's almost like the evolution of your psyche. If you're a creative person, there's this need to make stuff. But the definition of that widens as your desire to create turns into the ability to create turns into the ability to want to create an environment where other people can create.

I like my new role. There's a huge amount of freedom in not having to do a single job. The ability to talk to people, the ability to do outreach, to make connections outside of the building . . . that part is really rewarding. And if you think about ideas as something you have to get out in order to make room for more ideas, then with management, in a way, you can be more creative because you're dealing with more ideas. You're in the big part of everything, and that is so gratifying. You know a lot less, but you're learning so much more. You start to think about sitting there grinding it out on one idea at a time as really elemental or primitive. But you have to start with that. There's nothing like the sheer pleasure of making one thing. That's the essence of craft, which can lead to so much more.

ALICIA DOTTER

360 Senior Creative Director, Amazon

THE ADVICE I give to new managers is often the same I give to new moms. Don't feel bad if you don't love it at first; it's not easy. How could you expect to be good at something you've literally *never* done? Give it time, ask the moms (and managers) who you admire how *they* do it. What are their tips and tricks? And then suddenly one day you'll be sitting in a meeting, beaming with pride because one of your creatives just sold a campaign they worked *so* hard on. And you'll realize, "Ohhhhh, so *this* is what it's all about."

• • •

DUNCAN MILNER

Former Global Creative President, Media Arts Lab, MAL For Good

YOU NEED TO be open to being surprised. You're going to have ideas in your own head, and you can't help but formulate ideas on your own, but you have to be willing to be open to something you didn't expect. Once you can do that, then the job becomes really exciting. It's really cool to go into a meeting and see something you didn't expect.

RON RADZINER

President, Design Partner, Marmol Radziner Architects

I WOULD BROADLY advocate higher-level guidance versus getting into the weeds. If you do get into a high level of detail, you're probably going to frustrate the people under you and stifle their ability to produce good work. They are much more in it, day to day, than I am. They're discovering things that I wouldn't be able to see. I have to remember that and allow their projects to go places I didn't expect.

There are moments when we're hired to do a really exciting project and I want to do the whole thing, but more often than not the reality is I can't. I can do some sketches, but I have to hand it off to someone else to develop further. That's hard. I used to love getting into the granularity of detail, but now I like looking at the design and the big idea, and being able to

touch so many things that are getting built. I'm still able to experience just a little of what my staff are doing.

I think if you really need to design something completely by yourself, you need to find the appropriate project for that outlet. I designed the home I live in presently very much as a personal project. That level of involvement company-wide is impossible.

DAVID OYELOWO

Actor, *Selma*; Producer, *Come Away*; Director, *The Water Man*

YOU NEED TO recognize when to step back, and recognize when to step in. Leaders make the mistake of thinking their job is to consistently be seen as leading, as opposed to being someone who engenders confidence in the endeavor. You don't have to be leading in every moment. As Martin Scorsese said, "Ninety percent of directing is casting." Getting the right person for the role is crucial.

In my experience, having been led and been a leader, it's important to have someone who is self-aware and self-confident enough to allow people to flourish and thrive, and who has a clear vision of what they want. I have been directed by people who, probably coming from a place of insecurity, made the fundamental mistake of telling an incredible cast and crew—hair, makeup, everyone involved—precisely how to do their job. It never leads to a good film or a good project because you're taking the joy out of the thing you've tasked people to do, and taking away their ability to confidently do their tasks.

I think the worst thing you can do as a leader is micromanage people in a way that takes away their agency. When you hire people who have a level of expertise that is likely to elevate what you mean for them to do, it allows for an environment where you're not having to rush in to help, and empowers people to be the best version of themselves. You can still be there as a facilitator and as a sounding board, but you have effectively allowed them be the solution to any problem they may come up with.

In directing my first feature film, I never felt the need to save someone or solve something for them. I never found it necessary to go in and tell people how to do their jobs. If you hired the right people, they will take what you've given them to the next level, and the only times they're going to need you is to make sure they haven't gone too far with what you've said, or that you still feel like what they're doing is still synonymous with your vision.

to be irrational or emotional arguments in order to make something that you think is beautiful, worthwhile, and necessary. And you're often confronted with people who are arguing from a position of time or a position of money. So, as a director, it's your job to fight like hell to say, "We have to do this, and we have to do it this way."

Now that I run a studio and have a team of creative executives that work with me, I can no longer take that autocratic approach. I've learned this the hard way. If I'm obstinate or demanding, like I was when I was a director, I'll lose their respect and their best creativity. It's a quick way to lose that very valuable sense of teamwork, camaraderie, and investment.

Over the years, I've learned to listen more. I encourage people to challenge me. That's really hard to do when you're the boss. In my mind, I always think I have the best path to a solution, but now I'm learning that their path is better because they're going to have to do it. It's essential to avoid "yes people" and to allow talented, creative people to have their autonomy.

DAVIS GUGGENHEIM

Producer and Director, *Deadwood*, *Melrose Place*, *An Inconvenient Truth*, *Waiting for Superman*, *It Might Get Loud*

WHEN YOU'RE A director of a movie, you're in charge and most people don't dispute that. It's your job to tell people what to do all day. Often, you're making what seems

• • •

WHAT THEY SAID, summarized:

- Don't try to be the talent and the manager. Pick one role.
- The role of leader takes getting used to.
- Artists don't like to be challenged by management or compete with them. There's only room for one artist in the studio.
- You need to evolve your perspective and look for satisfaction in seeing others succeed.
- There is gratification in being a big part in everything, and not just one thing.
- It takes time to appreciate a hands-off, managerial role.
- Be open to being surprised and seeing things you didn't expect.
- Know when to step back and know when to step in.
- Micromanaging takes away people's agency.
- You'll make people unhappy or lose them if you push your agenda too hard.
- Let people attempt to solve things on their own.
- Find personal projects that feed your creative urges.

Maintain a Culture of

CONSISTENCY
CONSISTENCY
CONSISTENCY
CONSISTENCY
CONSISTENCY
CONSISTENCY
CONSISTENCY

MAINTAIN
A CULTURE OF
CONSISTENCY.

Near the top of the frustration food chain sits inconsistent feedback. Nothing is more dispiriting to a creative person than getting told one thing by their creative leader only to be told something contradictory later, especially if you've been busy creating or revising based on the first opinion. You have every right to change your mind about something, but if it becomes habitual, or is viewed as a lack of conviction, it can be caustic.

Try to stay as consistent as possible with your viewpoints and feedback. The more that people can map back to the way you think or what you previously said, the happier they'll be. If people know you don't like physical comedy, puns, the color chartreuse, or omniscient first person narration, then you should always hate physical comedy, puns, chartreuse, and omniscient first person narration.

You have every right to change your mind or like something new; just be aware of the consequences of conflicting messaging. Not knowing where the bull's-eye is located and consistently being asked to hit it will lead to frustration, and frustration leads to disengagement. A consistent perspective will earn the trust of the people who work for you and will ultimately lead to happier, more productive creative teams.

• • •

MARGARET KEENE

Executive Creative Director, Mullen LA

THIS IS SOMETHING we all struggle with. I try not to be an absolutist in my style and opinions. I don't want creatives to hold back because I have a bunch of issues they need to cater to. I've seen a lot of work bite the dust because a leader only likes puns, for instance. I really want them to own all the ways into an idea, as wild and impossible as they may be, and I reiterate this all the time. Follow strategy and then blow it up. Push me hard, especially if we have time to explore. Then, when we've given it every shot, we can be realistic with what moves forward.

I try to maintain conviction, focus, and a consistently clear direction, but some ideas are at the mercy of mitigating factors. You know the ones: the client changes, the planner realizes everyone's off strategy, the Super Bowl budget has been whittled down to a 250 x 250 banner ad. I try and be as honest with the teams about the journey ahead, and I try to explain any changes in attitude or receptivity.

Some folks lead on a "need to know" basis. Not me. I tell them everything. We're partners, and we need to move forward together and make the coolest shit we can. I'll make the heavy decisions, but I need my teams to know in their gut what to do, way before I get in the room.

TED PRICE

President and Founder, Insomniac Games

WHEN WE BUILD video games, we're often traveling into unknown territory. We're trying to do things that haven't been done before and so there's rarely a right answer to what we're attempting to accomplish. With that in mind, it's really easy to spend a lot of time second-guessing ourselves before we start building anything. This can be paralyzing.

So we have to be comfortable diving into the construction process, knowing things will change.

Since change tends to be uncomfortable for people, it's also really important for us to explain the *why* behind our decisions. That's an easy thing for people making decisions to forget. We have the reasons in our heads, but when we forget to explain the why, other team members think, "Wow, this person is really fickle; they're flip-flopping," or "They're making decisions with no real data to back it up."

Therefore, we push our designers, creative directors, and anyone in a leadership position to explain their rationale so that others have a chance to raise objections, question the motivations, and then eventually to buy into the decisions being made.

This helps to create a culture of consistency where, even if we *are* changing direction, the team understands that there's a well-thought-out reason for the change.

MATTHEW WARD

Creative Director, Cinematic Director, Bungie Games

I BELIEVE IT'S crucial to get early creative alignment on things so that everyone is clear on what our bull's-eye is. But, as much as we try to stick to that, sometimes changes are inevitable. Maybe you discover through your team's creative exploration that the initial direction was wrong. Maybe a new idea appears that strengthens the direction you were initially headed toward. Maybe there have been amendments to the project. Just know that changing course too late in any creative project is usually met with a negative effect on the team—no one likes to throw away great art.

WHAT THEY SAID, summarized:

- Maintain consistent and clear direction and feedback.
- People also appreciate consistency in communication.
- Being absolutist in your opinions, style, or taste could limit creative potential.
- In addition to giving consistent direction, make people aware of potential changes.
- Always give the *why* when making decisions.
- If you allow people to object and question your rationale, they are more likely to buy into it.
- Change is sometimes inevitable.

LESS PUSHING
MORE PULLING

LESS PUSHING,
MORE PULLING.

Creative people are used to pushing to get their ideas made. We have a vision of what we want and we fight to bring that vision to life with minimal compromise. We instruct teams on exactly what to make, then we force the work through the different channels, fighting off the naysayers or critics who want to chip away at the integrity of the idea, and in our minds, change things for the worse. Pushing, and pushing back, are second nature to us, and the minute someone says, "What if you—"

Shhh, just stop there. Not gonna happen.

Great ideas are definitely worth fighting for, and no great piece of work is born without a few minor skirmishes. But you'll experience more success by pulling people together in more collaborative ways versus strong-arming or trying to bypass them. Working with people, whether they're members of your team, other leaders within your company, the next layer of management, or clients, allows you to harness the power of different types of expertise, helps build advocacy, and could provide you with valuable insight. And by building consensus, gaining collective support and buy-in from everyone involved, you'll end up with more people who are also willing to push, which takes the burden off of you.

How you make things is just as important as *what* you make. As you consider the short-term gains of making something, consider the long-term costs of fighting to make it. Working with people on projects as opposed to working against them and creating adversarial relationships is going to be much better for you in the long run. People will be more engaged in the success of your project, and will be more likely to help on the next one. Next time you find yourself in the position of championing something, remember: you're stronger together.

• •

SAM BERGEN

Vice President, Global Brand Creative, Beats by Dr. Dre

BUILD CONSENSUS. I don't want to hedge conservatively, because I think that can result in mediocre work if you don't follow through. I always found, my entire life, that I've never done anything alone. It was the success of other people that helped me do anything. So, from a very early state in my career, it was always, "How do I figure out what other people are trying to accomplish to be able to get an idea through?"

We have nearly four million followers on Instagram, and we recently decided to delete our entire archive of content. We're starting over and changing everything. No more athletes. No more musicians. No more high-level parties you can't go to. It's a huge shift for us as a brand, since it's been our social presence for a while now. I don't know if it's going to work. I have theories for why we're doing this and I bought us about two years of runway to test and learn, and we'll know at the end if it was a good thing or bad thing. In that process, we might fall on our faces a few times and may have to issue an apology. But the

theories are a good thing to be testing. And I build consensus around whatever outcome might come, and then have a plan in place.

I brought in an external point of view who I didn't know whether would side on my thesis or not. The external point of view helped open up a lot of conversations and was the first step to getting everyone to say, "Okay, it's time to evolve and move on."

DAVIS GUGGENHEIM

Producer and Director, *Deadwood*, *Melrose Place*, *An Inconvenient Truth*, *Waiting for Superman*, *It Might Get Loud*

I'M NOW THE head of a studio where there are several executives and other directors (of movies I'm just producing). Being a director, where the structure of command and control is really clear, I pushed my agenda in the beginning. The problem was, this was making people unhappy: they didn't feel empowered, and some even left.

In one instance, I requested my executive team create a sizzle reel for a movie that was in production so that our investor and buyers would see its potential. My team advised against it, arguing that it was too early and that the people who were making the movie would react badly. But I made them do it, and they followed the order. Lo and behold, the sizzle was very unpopular. Even worse, my team felt like I didn't listen to them. And instead of lamenting what happened, they were like, "Yeah, we expected that." I learned you can get your team to do something they really don't want to do, but it's not worth doing if they're not invested and passionate about the result. Everyone wants to feel like they're being heard and that some idea isn't being shoved down their throat.

One way I try to counter that is to keep my words to a minimum in meetings, and listen to what people have to say. I wait for people to find the right path, and when I see them arrive at the answer on their own, that's when I stop in and say, "That's it." It's like catching a fish—you're waiting for a little nibble, that thing you agree with, and then you pull on the line. Because the ideas originate from everyone else in the room, they feel more ownership, and they feel like I'm listening instead of dictating.

BRIAN MILLER

Creative Director, The Walt Disney Company/ Global Marketing

I LOVE THE feeling of being a part of an idea that is so infectious that others in the agency—and with the clients—want to be a part of it. They want to help build it, share it, and make it better. It's a great feeling.

Sometimes the idea itself doesn't have this effect on its own. That's when you need to ask others to join in or to pull them in. The difference is in how you present it. I like to find a way to make it more of a "we have an idea here that we know can be more. I'd love to have your thoughts on this." Sometimes it's as simple as that.

WHAT THEY SAID, summarized:

- Building consensus helps drive success.
- Consensus shows the power of the idea.
- Bringing other people in can help grow ideas and expand their reach.
- Pushing too hard can affect workplace happiness and stifle creativity.
- Pulling people in allows people to feel ownership of ideas.

FALLING ON
TOO MANY
SWORDS
KILLS
CREDIBILITY

FALLING ON TOO MANY SWORDS KILLS **CREDIBILITY.**

No matter what creative field you're in, at some point you've probably had to defend an idea or the execution of an idea well past the point of normal advocacy. You've had to fall on your sword and risk your reputation, or even your job. Maybe you won. Maybe you lost. Hopefully you won.

Indeed, some things are worth fighting for. But if you fight for too much, too often, and with too much vigor, it can come at a cost. When you fall on your sword for something, you're showing such a strong creative conviction that it makes other people question themselves. When you fall on too many, it makes other people question *you*. You risk being perceived as someone who is inflexible, dogmatic, combative, immature, or biased beyond reason. As a creative leader, you want to be seen as pragmatic, a team player, and someone who is willing to consider the opinions of others. Falling on too many swords incrementally robs your arguments of their strength. People will give less credence to what you have to say, even when you actually do have a strong case for something.

Pick the moments to fall on your sword carefully. Decide if it's truly worth it, and if the proposed change will truly impact the project or if it will just be a detail that only you notice. Other factors to consider are the chance you have of changing people's minds, and who you're up against. Will they take exception to your hard-line stance? How influential are they, and what is the potential downside? If the risk outweighs the reward, and if the short-term gains end up costing you even more later, you might consider sheathing your sword and saving that opportunity for a later date.

• •

MARCELLA COAD

Creative Director, Amazon

CULTURE IS A really important aspect of if, when, and how often you should fall on your sword. If you're in a culture where failure is accepted, and challenging viewpoints is expected behavior, then perhaps you can fall on swords with greater frequency. It really depends how open people are to mistakes or being wrong.

But you can't just fall on a sword based on a gut feeling. Here at Amazon, if you're going to fight for things, you have to have a solid bedrock of data, strategy, research, anecdotal information, or proof points to back up your argument. And it helps to have a team that's equally invested to back you up. You won't get very far on, "I really like it," or, "Just trust me." And a solo mission probably won't go so well.

To me, fighting for ideas is a learned skill. I think it depends on the tone of how you defend your work. You can do it in a persuasive way, or in a way that can come across as combative. And you need to take into account subjectivity and different taste levels, which, like it or not, are sometimes better and sometimes worse. And you gotta know the people involved. Are they open to being challenged? The art is knowing when it's right to fight for that idea, casting decision, or music track . . . and when it's going to really piss someone off.

As I've gotten higher and higher up, I see fewer and fewer people fighting relentlessly to save their work. They might have been inflexible back in the day, but they seem to choose their battles more carefully now. And from what I can tell, the senior folks who fight for work too frequently tend to get weeded out pretty quick.

Interestingly, one of the operating principles at Amazon is having the backbone to "disagree and commit." They believe that, as a leader, it's your obligation to challenge decisions if you disagree, and not to compromise just because it's easier. So, to them, it's just as important to fall on a sword *against* something as it is to fall on one *for* something.

MATTHEW WARD

Creative Director, Cinematic Director, Bungie Games

ANY CREATIVE SHOULD be willing to fall on my sword if they see a huge opportunity, or to the contrary, huge danger up ahead. As a director, it could be getting a certain shot, or picking the proper camera angle, or making sure the lighting is exactly what you want. You weigh the feedback and you listen to people, but if you're still feeling strong about something, and experience has taught you that what you believe is probably right, then there is nothing wrong with standing by your opinion, come hell or high water.

If you're going to hold fast to an opinion, there's a lot you need to assess. You need to weigh the severity of the request you're making. You need to understand potential outcomes, good or bad, based on past experience. And you absolutely need to know who you're talking to and what their reactions could be. If you've already established a trusting relationship with the people involved, that definitely helps the validity of your voice.

WHAT THEY SAID, summarized:

- Make sure your culture is accepting of challenging viewpoints. Know the people involved. Consider the dynamics of the room.
- Choose your battles. Arm yourself with information that helps you make your case.
- There's an art in knowing when to fight and how to do it.
- Sometimes it's important to fall on your sword *against* something.
- Understand potential outcomes.
- Trust definitely helps.

TAKE RISKS

BUT MITIGATE DISASTERS

TAKE RISKS
BUT MITIGATE DISASTERS.

Let's face it. There's risk involved in everything we do. A movie or show might not land with audiences. A marketing campaign might miss sales targets. After you present ideas for that new logo, new building, new edit, new cookie recipe, new greeting card, or a new mobile app, the client or public could very well respond with a big ole meh. It happens.

Taking a risk and failing means going back to the drawing board, but a disaster is much harder to recover from. Disasters can lead to people losing their jobs, companies being fired, clients going under, the gateway to Hell opening and unleashing a horde of demons and condemning mankind to an eternal damnation. (At least, I always assume that last thing will happen if the Super Bowl ad I do for Honda doesn't perform well.)

It's important to assess the levels of risk associated with each project, and to pressure test your work for vulnerabilities. You also need to be honest about risks with clients so they're not caught off guard if things don't go as planned. What are the client expectations? Where are potential issues? Are there guardrails you can put up to protect yourself? Does it hit on any racial or cultural hot buttons? What is the importance of the project to the company, and how might that factor into failure? Remember, the more important the project, the greater the chance of it being a *Gigli*-level disaster if it doesn't work out. (Then again . . . Bennifer turned out just fine.)

JON IKEDA

VP, Acura Brand Officer
and former Lead Designer, Acura

HONDA IS KNOWN as an innovation company, but there's no innovation without risk. They live next to each other. Innovation is about being first and going into places where others aren't brave enough to play in. You need to get comfortable being uncomfortable. Creative people more naturally live there, more so than others.

Honda is an engineering company with a lot of R&D, engineers, and salespeople. They love to communicate with each other with numbers, graphs, and charts, and there's a lot of logic guiding their decisionmaking. But there has to be a balance between logic and creativity. When I was on the design team, our job was to convince people who live in the logic world to look at a car design differently. It's like *Star Trek*: the two main characters were Kirk and Spock. One is completely consumed with logic and thinks that emotion can take you to bad places; and then the other guy was all intuition, guts, and glory.

We have to have good balance in order to be successful and prevent disaster. If you did *Star Trek* with just Kirk, you'd fly the *Enterprise* into the sun in episode three and that would be it. And if you did it with just Spock, it would probably be incredibly boring, slow, and repetitive. Everything would be tremendously cautious, and they'd never go anywhere. And no one wants to watch a show about "paralysis by analysis."

At the end, there's no amount of data that's going to guarantee anything 100 percent or predict the future. At some point, you're going to have to believe in your heart and pull the trigger. That's what Kirk does. Intuition based on experience.

It's becoming more of an issue lately because there's so much more data now than ever before. And people use it like a crutch. If you wait to sort out all of the data, until you're almost 100 percent sure and confident that it's going to be successful, then you're not going to be innovative, because by that time someone else has already done it. And if you rely on just the data for your creative idea, then it's probably going to be incredibly safe and expected. Everyone is looking at the same data. The one that can be most creative with the data early will be the winner.

It's riskier not to take risks. If you don't, you won't be an innovator. For me, it's critical that creative people not just go in there and be crazy Kirks, but understand it is a balance, and on certain occasions, when time allows, it's better to Spock something to make people comfortable. Balance.

• • •

SAM OLIVER

Group Creative Director, Apple

WHEN YOU'RE A creative person and not the leader, you don't care as much about the consequences. You're willing to take the risks because you're not paying for it or necessarily taking the fall for it if things go wrong. And as a creative person, your whole future is based on your creative work. If you just do average work you're probably not going to go very far. So you have to go for it, and the biggest risk is not to. I think that it's an easy choice at that stage of your career.

But as time goes on, you become more accountable and that potential for disaster is more present in your mind. Before coming to Apple, when I was a creative and producing commercials, there were always clients and account managers on set to make sure we were getting proper coverage of the product. After coming to Apple as a creative director, I had to be more like those clients and account directors. I had to be the one leaning in, making sure we get everything and that product looks amazing, because I'm the one who's accountable. So, quite simply, the more your head's on the line, the more you prepare for all the outcomes and potential solutions.

I think the team dynamic is really important when it comes to risk-taking. We have many conversations at Apple about the work, and often ask, "Is that Apple?" or, "Is that something Apple should do?" And often the answer might be, "No, that doesn't feel right." But then sometimes it forces us to ask, "It's not something we've done before but maybe it's what we should be doing." And then there's a debate, and we assess the risk. But it's usually a group decision and we all hold hands (metaphorically) and say, "Okay, let's do it." I think you need to be in a culture where you have that joint accountability, and whoever the decisionmakers are, it's important to look each other in the eye and go, "If it goes wrong, it goes wrong. But we're all in this together."

DAVID OYELOWO

Actor, *Selma*; Producer, *Come Away*; Director, *The Water Man*

THERE'S A VERY ugly tension between creativity and commerce. As a creative person you want to feel groundbreaking, you want to be critically acclaimed, you want to be moving the needle. Often, commerce doesn't want to take the risks. They're more concerned about the bottom line and not coloring outside the margins so much that you risk alienating anyone. These motivations are very much in conflict with each other. How do you create something of value when you also have to make something palatable to risk-averse companies who are more focused on eyeballs and profitability?

The only way a studio accepts risk are when they themselves feel the belief and the passion that you have for the project. If you are projecting that you are willing to stake your life on your work, and if you let them know your intention is to make something that will ultimately benefit them, that will lower the risk in their minds. If your client, or the studio head, or production company president, has been in their business long enough, they know there's risk involved in everything they make. What they're trying to do is mitigate as much risk as possible, and one way to do it is to hitch their wagon to people with the kind of passion that gives them confidence.

WHAT THEY SAID, summarized:

- Get comfortable being uncomfortable.
- You need to balance logic and creativity to avoid disaster.
- At the end of the day, you need to employ intuition based on experience.
- Don't let data stop you from doing great work, fast.
- It's riskier not to take risks.
- Leaders are more accountable and need to assess risk levels.
- The support and accountability of all decisionmakers is important when taking a risk.
- Belief and passion help convince people to take risks.

Awards should be the fortuitous result of smart work, not the goal.

AWARDS SHOULD BE THE **FORTUITOUS** RESULT OF SMART WORK, NOT THE GOAL.

f you're in a creative field where awards matter, and you work with clients, then listen up: your personal desire to create award-winning work should never usurp the need to do the right work for your clients. You should always be working with their best interests in mind. It's okay to try to push clients out of their comfort zones with breakthrough or disruptive ideas, but the rationale should be specific to the client's brand or needs, not because it's award bait and can earn you shiny new hardware for your mantel.

As a creative leader, awards should generally be the fortuitous result of smart work that, first and foremost, does its intended job. If it can do that, and then it wins awards because it was brilliant, beautiful, or effective, then kudos. But be very careful. If a client thinks that you're trying to sell them work for your personal benefit and not theirs, it will erode whatever trust you've established. And trust, as we've discussed earlier, is everything.

• • •

TIM LEAKE

SVP/Chief Marketing & Innovation Officer,
RPA Advertising

I WORK IN the advertising industry thanks to the Energizer Bunny.

When I first saw that campaign, it lit up my young, hadn't-yet-decided-what-I-want-to-do-when-I-grow-up brain. It surprised me, made me laugh, told me something relevant about the product, and helped me remember (and prefer) the Energizer brand, over and over again. It was huge. And naturally, it won every ad industry award at the time.

Thanks to a healthy balance of determination and utter ignorance that failure was a possibility, my first job as a junior copywriter was at Chiat\Day, working on—yep—the Energizer Bunny campaign. I was excited to be in this industry. I loved the notion of using creativity to make things people would love, and that would also help grow businesses. What an amazing alignment of goals!

But the bunny lied.

In reality, I found those goals rarely aligned. It turns out that creative people were often relentlessly and exclusively focusing their energy on winning awards. While I was striving to create work that would help build our clients' business, my creative coworkers on Energizer were getting well rewarded for their efforts. As a still-impressionable young writer, I thought I must be doing it wrong.

The sad truth is that sometimes what's in the best interest of your clients isn't the same as what's going to win big at award shows like the Cannes Lions. Especially when you're competing against work that isn't weighed down by things such as a realistic media format, a realistic production budget, or a client that actually needs to sell something. And it's gotten worse over time. It's painfully obvious that most of the work that wins in award shows was developed only so that it could be entered in award shows. Meanwhile—and not coincidentally, I think—there is a shrinking number of great creative campaigns that resonate with people and popular culture in a way that drives business success.

But you know what? That right there is a massive opportunity, especially for you talented folks making the transition from creative doer to creative leader. You have the opportunity to refocus your creative firepower on what matters again.

When you become a creative director, you receive an amazing gift—you get credit no matter what. You now get to decide what's important, and you no longer have to play the game. You get to realign creative and marketing objectives if you choose to. And you *should* choose to. Because now you're in the second act of your career, and now's the time to think about longevity. You don't want to find yourself irrelevant by the age of forty-five.

Ever notice that popularity in high school is a pretty crappy predictor of success as an adult? Well, it can be the same with winning awards early in your career. I've seen many award-winning creatives find themselves frustratingly out of work as they get older because they never realized there's more to this career than the awards game.

Successful creative leaders have long careers because they understand the need to align our objectives. They understand that great creativity is a competitive advantage for a brand's business. So embrace your new power. You have the opportunity to look beyond the awards game and focus on what's right. Your career will thank you. Your clients will thank you. Do it right. You'll win more awards this way anyhow.

SAM OLIVER

Group Creative Director, Apple

I STRUGGLE WITH the whole awards culture. But the problem is, when you're a creative person in this industry, you're often judged by how many awards you've won. It's the way to get a pay raise, to get a promotion, and to get a new job. When I was in London growing up in this business, it was very important to get awards, and you knew the kind of work you'd have to do to get one. It wasn't always the effective work, or the right work. It was clean, and it wasn't encumbered by product, phone numbers, or calls to action. I think awards can potentially hurt the work because creative people end up making things based on what they think an award show jury will like versus "what the right thing to do is." But, having said that, I think they do need to exist because you need to reward and encourage completely new thinking and ways of solving things. The problem comes when people overly fixate on them instead of focusing on the wider picture.

When I came to Apple, one of my big reliefs was that awards weren't as important. Yes, Apple's marketing wins them, but our eye isn't on that. It's on just trying to do good work. I'm a lot more comfortable in that arena, and actually, I think most creative people are. It's such a big pressure to live in that world. However, it's important to note that, even as a leader, creativity is still part of how you're being evaluated. Did you keep clients, did you grow revenue, and did you creatively excel? You're still held accountable, but it's a wider accountability.

● ● ●

WHAT THEY SAID, summarized:

- Creative leaders need to refocus on driving business goals, first and foremost.
- Being a creative leader allows you to rise above the game of getting noticed.
- You ensure career longevity when your work is effective as well as creative.
- The danger is when you over-fixate on awards vs. seeing the wider picture.
- Start by trying to do good work that is right for the job.
- Even though awards are not the focal point, creativity is often an evaluation tool.

Work rarey sells itself

WORK RARELY SELLS ITSELF.

Creative people aren't exactly natural salespeople. In fact, based on my experience, creative types are typically more emotional and insecure introverts who are better at coming up with the idea than selling its virtues. Sales jobs are typically reserved for the charming, fearless, undaunted conversationalists who enjoy the challenge of convincing someone to buy.

We got into our respective creative fields because we enjoyed making things, but now that we've risen up through the ranks, or because we run our own companies, we find ourselves in the dubious position of peddling our wares. And there's a great deal of pressure on us to succeed. Our business depends on it, and there are people relying on us to sell work, from those who helped make it, to the people who run the company, to the people you might be pitching.

Go in prepped and ready to go. Know the assignment, the audience you're presenting to, and the work you're showing. Determine the problem and focus your pitch on how you can help solve it. Don't simply present your ideas and expect people to naturally understand why it's great. Explain the genius of it. And don't just "say" your ideas. Use that creative passion to romance the hell out of them and capture your audience's imaginations. And remember, as a creative leader, it's important to romance ideas even when they're your team's and not your own.

You can make the best thing in the world. But how you sell it could be the difference between "start over" and "I love it."

• •

BILL WESTBROOK

CEO, No Fences Brand Consulting; former President, Executive Creative Director, Fallon Worldwide

THE TRANSITION FROM creative person to creative director brings fresh pressures and responsibilities, some obvious and some not so obvious. In the less-obvious category is that you're no longer free to complain about clients not buying your best work. More than anyone else in the agency, you own that little problem. It's heavy, but as a new creative director, you're suddenly wholly or significantly responsible for your agency's creative reputation going forward.

I often tell young creative directors that creating great work is only the beginning of the battle. Selling great work—and keeping it sold through production—is arguably harder. It's particularly hard if you have clients who don't want what you want and who have patterns of behaving that make it difficult, if not impossible, for great work to survive into production. The list of possibilities is long: layers of approval, endless rounds of work, differing definitions of "great" work, or the agency losing control as it makes its way up the client food chain. These are all client-management issues that must be solved.

Here are some examples of potential problems you might want to consider addressing:

1) Having to present too much work. Almost inevitably, the client will choose weaker or safer or more-expected work from the buffet.

2) Being forced to present work over the phone. The creative director loses leverage in this scenario, because the force of their belief or passion is essentially nullified. Plus, bad clients mute.

3) Not being allowed to present the work to the real decisionmakers. When the client is representing the work upstairs, the agency is powerless in most cases to influence the decision. It is the rare client you'd trust to present your work to their boss.

XANTHE WELLS

Senior Director, Global Executive Creative Director, Devices & Services, Google

I THINK THAT advertising agencies often make the mistake of telling people that they need to be showmen in order to sell work. I've learned that a lot of clients don't want showmanship or flare. They want good creative ideas that are presented with humility and, more importantly, by someone who shows they're willing and able to listen to feedback.

A lot of creatives don't leave room for meaningful feedback sessions when they present work, and often fill the time wall-to-wall with their own voices rather than those of the people on the other side.

DAVIS GUGGENHEIM

Producer and Director, *Deadwood, Melrose Place, An Inconvenient Truth, Waiting for Superman, It Might Get Loud*

I DON'T THINK I started out as a particularly good salesman, but because I needed work, I had no choice but to become one. Every idea and every job required me to sell it. Coming up with an idea for film and going off and making it is one form of creativity, but convincing an investor or studio to part with their money and finance your film is another one.

When I started out pitching movies, I would focus on making a rational argument, but that's not what any executive wants. They want to feel your excitement and imagine something so great that they can't say no. I'm always trying to touch on that "magic," to make them feel like they're sitting in the movie theater or in front of the TV, and let them forget about business for the moment.

WHAT THEY SAID, summarized:

- As a leader, you are responsible for your workplace's creative reputation.
- Selling great work is often harder than creating it.
- Attempt to sell work in person, with the decisionmakers in attendance.
- Present with humility. Avoid too much showmanship or flair.
- Leave room for meaningful feedback or discussion.
- Selling is another form of creativity that we need to get comfortable with.
- Sell your excitement about the work. People want to feel how much you love it.

Keep making things
if making things
makes you happy

KEEP MAKING THINGS IF MAKING THINGS MAKES YOU HAPPY.

Just because you're managing others doesn't mean you have to stop making things yourself. If making things makes you happy, then make things! If you enjoy painting, paint! If you like to direct, film something! It you have a penchant for poetry, scribble away! If pottery stokes your creative fires, go buy a lathe! If you want to write a better book on creative leadership than this one, do it! A creative outlet can give you a means to make things, and can do miracles for your mental health and overall well-being.

Staying creative isn't just beneficial to you, it's actually beneficial to the people working for you, too. When you have a means of creative expression that provides you self-satisfaction, you won't be as likely to try to prove your worth making things alongside your team. You'll be less likely to compete with your team on their assignments and needlessly refashion their ideas. You'll have your own projects, they'll have their own projects, and everyone will create happily ever after.

. . .

AVA DUVERNAY

Executive Producer, *Queen Sugar*;
Director, *When They See Us, Selma, A Wrinkle in Time*

IF YOU'RE A creative person, you have to know when you're being fed and when you need to be fed. And if you're starving creatively because you've taken on "leadership or managerial roles," that starvation manifests in different ways, one of which is you strangle the creativity of others. You're not the maker anymore. I've seen people who try to inhabit that role, who strangle or inhibit opportunity, forward movement, or ideas for the people that should be making and creating. We need to have the confidence to let others step into that role and the wherewithal to say, "I need to be fed right now and I need to make something for myself." I think some of the most prolific makers of television and film are folks that are producing for other people but still making their own things. Look at my friend J.J. Abrams: his name is on all kinds of things. He's producing for all kinds of people. But he's still actively making his own stuff. And when he's talking to artists, it's more eye-to-eye.

I would be a lot more comfortable, relaxed, and make a lot more money if I stopped making my own stuff and just tried to make a hundred more Avas. But I know that's not going to make me happy. I need to be fed. For me, actively doing things allows me to give good advice, good leadership, good protection, and good space to people.

JEFF GILES

Executive Editor, *Vanity Fair*;
Author, *The Edge of Everything*

ON A REALLY simple level, it's like a captain who was once a player, where everyone knows that you've done it yourself and that you're still doing it, and you know exactly how hard it is. I think it gives you more empathy and more credibility in people's eyes. I've known editors who can't write or don't write, but who are fantastic editors. I've never understood it, but they do exist.

Writing something that has your name on it is a totally different experience. Writing, as miserable and hard as it is, would be hard for me to stop altogether.

JOE RUSSO

Executive Producer, *Community*; Director,
Avengers: Endgame; Founder, Bullitt Productions

EVEN THOUGH WE'RE managers, we're still artists first and creators first.

TED PRICE

President and Founder, Insomniac Games

GAMES ARE FUN to make, and so when you see a problem, it's really tempting to want to just jump in and start making fixes. But if you're a leader, your job is not to do someone else's job. It's to empower them to do their job better.

One challenge we often run into is that those who say they want to lead often have a hard time actually making the leap from implementing to delegating. It's easy to raise your hand and say, "I want a position that involves more responsibility and more compensation." But when you're also an expert craftsperson, it takes a real leap of faith to stay hands off and trust others to do things just as well. What we tell our leaders is that by *not* taking up the craft they become "force multipliers" and can effect far more positive change. By trusting their teams to make the right fixes, to solve problems, and to take ownership of creation, leaders can focus on the bigger picture and moreover help each team member grow through regular guidance.

WHAT THEY SAID, summarized:

- Don't let your hunger to be creative rob your team of their opportunities.
- When you feel the need to be creative, step away and make something for yourself.
- Actively doing things for yourself can make you a better leader.
- Being a creator gives you more empathy and credibility in people's eyes.
- You can be a leader but still consider yourself an artist first.
- Going from maker to leader requires a difficult mental leap and isn't for everyone.
- Be sure you want the position and not just the title and a higher salary.

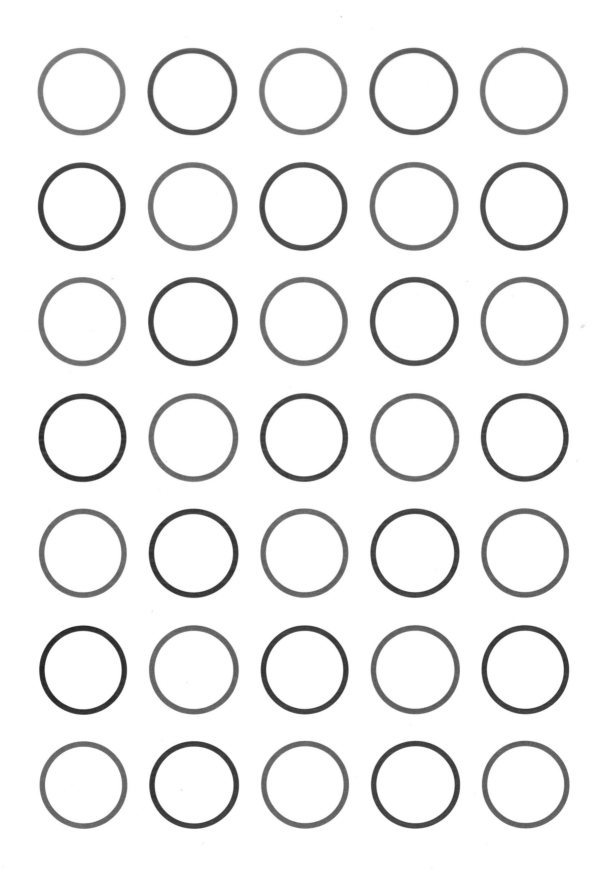

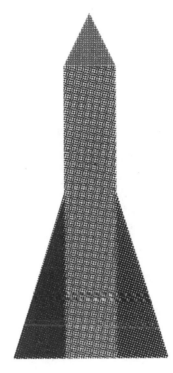

THE CAREER

SECTION 5
THE CAREER

We'd all love long, satisfying, storied careers in our chosen fields. The kind they honor at gala events where old cronies share embarrassing stories from the glory days and the next generation of creative stars shower you with praise and talk about how "your work has had such a huge influence on their own." Yep, sure would be nice.

Alas, nothing is guaranteed. Technological changes and shifting media have brought on a state of continual flux, and as a result, the need for constant adaptation. On top of that, the merciless pace and competitive environments of many creative industries often force people out prematurely. And the more senior and well paid we are, the more vulnerable we become when there's a downturn, economic uncertainty, or budget cuts. Point being, long careers can easily be cut short. Sorry to be a buzzkill.

(Cue sad piano soundtrack) I've been in the advertising business for two decades and recently left the familiar confines and cadence of the advertising agency world to become a creative lead at Facebook Reality Labs. I've seen the constant churn that comes from a demanding and subjective career. I've seen tumult and turnover as innovation, recessions, client departures, and evolving industry models have felled talented friends of mine, forcing them to endure long, anxiety-inducing periods of joblessness, or to uproot their families and move to other cities, or to even change their careers. I have watched the ageism/relevancy issue play out, and have seen senior creative people forced out or demoted to more menial positions. And I've seen the sometimes difficult adjustment creative people make after they've left the business. As Rick Colby, former CCO of Colby Dentsu, and a former creative leader of mine, once told me, "Enjoy the fun and energy of leading a creative department. When you retire, it's a feeling that's hard to replace."

(cue hopeful string ensemble) So how can we make ourselves relevant for years to come in this ever-evolving world? How do we protect ourselves from being let go, at any stage of our career? How do we approach the search for our next great job? And how do we keep our sanity amid all the daily madness?

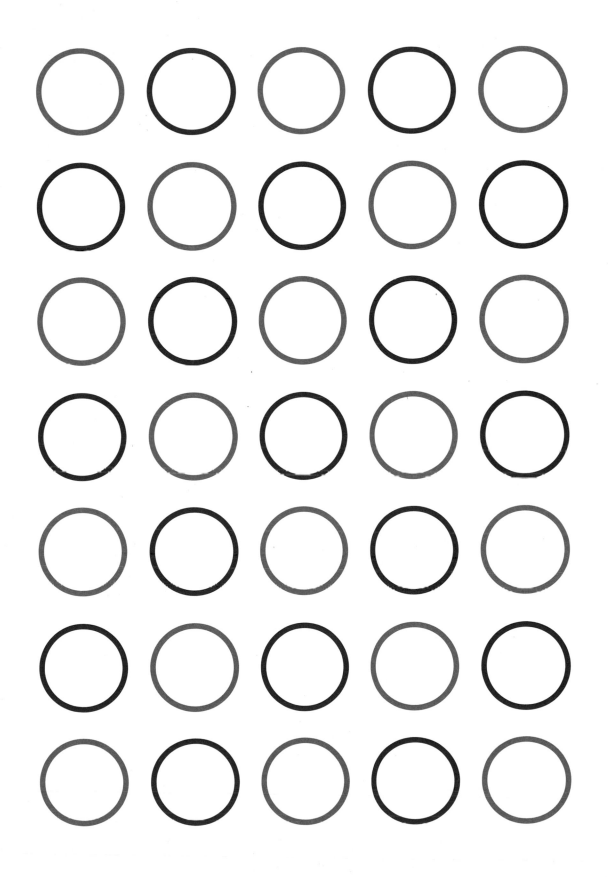

When it comes to your

job   career

be selfless   be selfish

WHEN IT COMES TO YOUR JOB,
BE SELFLESS.

When it comes to your career, be selfish.

f I haven't made it apparent enough already, this isn't just about you anymore. At work, you need to be a super-dedicated, loyal, selfless, and supportive leader to the people who work for you. It's all about your team. It's your job to help them develop their creative talents, champion their work, give them room to grow, shield them from the bureaucratic nonsense that would stifle their creativity, and advocate on their behalf so that they can become the next great industry leaders.

But . . .

. . . if you have the opportunity to take another job that offers you things you're looking for that you're not currently getting—professional growth, a more generous salary, a shorter commute, a better work/life balance, the chance to do even better work than you're doing now—then there's nothing wrong with looking out for yourself. Your career trajectory matters, too. And being selfish about it is okay.

One thing to note: selflessness and selfishness are not wholly separate from each other. We can be selfless at our jobs while selfishly looking for a new one. But while you're searching or going through the interview process, you should still be fully committed to the people and projects that are depending on you, until the end of your last day. Your team deserves it, and it keeps the door open for potentially going back down the road. And let's face it: they'll definitely want you back.

SAM OLIVER

Group Creative Director, Apple

WORKING FOR A company is a transactional relationship. They pay you to do a job that takes a lot of effort and you give them everything you can. There's parity between employee and employer, and you shouldn't feel guilty if you feel it's better for your career to move on.

At the same time, I believe you should always be decent to the people around you, the people you work for and work with. If I leave a company, I always try to leave at the right time, when it's good for the company and not just for me, so I don't put them in a bad situation during a big project. It's such a small world, as well. If you're a jerk, everyone is going to know about it and it's going to follow you wherever you go.

SCOTT TRATTNER

Former VP, Executive Creative Director, Facebook; former Executive Director, TBWA\Media Arts Lab

I WORKED ON the Apple account for ten years and just did five years at Facebook. I truly believe in servant leadership and putting the team in front of myself. When I went to Facebook, I learned that there's so much accountability to my team, and every day I gave 100 percent to them and their work.

But part of the reason why I took a year off from my role at Facebook was to nourish the artistic side of myself. I got to a place in my career where I was wondering, "Was this time well spent?" I grew up in the seventies with hippies. My background was in fine art. I was an artist before I was in advertising and marketing. And, to be candid, there was a part of me that was lost during this period: the curiosity around adjacent things that I liked doing outside my day job, like photography and art, because I was pouring everything into what I was doing at work. Leaving allowed me to reconnect with my artistic practice.

MATTHEW WARD

Creative Director, Cinematic Director, Bungie Games

WE NEED TO absolutely pour our heart and soul into our current gigs, but as artists we need to make sure we're staying creative and being fulfilled. Creativity is like a drug. And we need to make sure we're always getting the proper dosage.

WHAT THEY SAID, summarized:

- Your team depends on you.
- As a leader, you need to give 100 percent to your team.
- However, it's important to put your personal satisfaction first.
- You shouldn't feel guilty for exploring other opportunities.
- Try to leave at the right time, when the team and projects are in a good place.
- It's a small world. Try not to leave your team in a bad situation.

Keep working on You V.2

KEEP WORKING
ON YOU V.2.

Over the course of your career, you'll continually be faced with new challenges. All. The. Time. Just as an athlete requires conditioning to stay at the top of their game, you need to keep pace with an ever-changing industry, continue to expand your skill sets, and work on strengthening any weaknesses you have.

Maybe you're not the sharpest presenter. Maybe your client or department management skills need honing. Maybe your aren't particularly adept on a relevant software tool. Or all the above. Don't let your title or importance to a company make you too complacent or cavalier. Take a class or a workshop if you need one. Identify the problem before a supervisor or a recruiter at a potential new job does and says, "You're great but . . ."

On top of mastering the skills important to your leadership position, improve yourself in ways that help you stay current with your industry. With media platforms continually transforming and new technology continuing to emerge, change is a constant and inevitable aspect to our jobs. As your specific industry evolves, it's important to evolve with it. Adopt a mindset of lifelong learning. Build the relevant skills and understanding that make you invaluable, today and tomorrow. In other words, stay hungry, never get too comfortable, and never stop kicking ass.

• • •

AVA DUVERNAY

Executive Producer, Queen Sugar;
Director, When They See Us, Selma, A Wrinkle in Time

IN ORDER TO lead others, you have to know how to do the job yourself. The disconnect comes when, as a leader, you supervise the people doing it and you become out of touch with the doing, with the making, with the creation, with the art, with the imaginative piece of it. I've seen it happen with folks where it starts to get cushy and you start to work from your memory of things, and their experience is not evolving. Their experiences are from years ago, and things are changing every day. And so, if you're not in the trenches making it, or you're not respecting the people who are to the point that they're looking at things that are now past you, then I think it becomes difficult to be offering valuable leadership.

Yes, there's a type of leader that says, "I don't do this anymore, but I'm going to give you the space to do it and I'm going to block and tackle and protect." But too often we're asking people to move from one space to another and they're iterating off old assumptions and old experience.

SAM BERGEN

Vice President, Global Brand Creative, Beats by Dr. Dre

THERE ARE SO MANY fronts and faces and aspects to being a leader that very few people, if any, are born as true natural leaders, and those who are find out very quickly. But I would say for 99.9 percent of us out there, we're not natural leaders. It's a skill like anything else. You break down any personality tests, and although they're about complementary skill sets, you still have weaknesses that require strengthening.

I'm actually quite introverted and quiet, but this is the job. I've had to overcome being very quiet, thoughtful, and reserved, and be more vivacious and more inspirational. When I was younger, my friends would often joke that I was a bit robotic, and since nobody wants a robot as their boss, I had to really focus and work on changing those things that I didn't think helped me as a leader.

If you want to be a great leader and impact things at scale, you have to work on aspects of your personal weaknesses.

SCOTT TRATTNER

Former VP, Executive Creative Director, Facebook;
former Executive Director, TBWA\Media Arts Lab

IT'S REALLY IMPORTANT in my life, career, and whatever I'm doing that there's curiosity connected to it. As our industry has evolved along with the changing modalities around it, it's very hard from a strategic perspective to feel like I should learn this because that is changing, or I should sharpen that because it will make me more effective. I find it hard to motivate around those realizations. It's about curiosity. That opens a pathway I can step through. And if that isn't part of that equation, it's really tough for me to motivate. I try to minimize the things I have to do and maximize the things that are about curiosity.

But I'm a professional person, and if I have to learn something, I'll do it. A big part of my last job at Facebook was a deep understanding of metrics and analytics and how to measure creativity. I have an MFA in painting. There couldn't be something further away from who I am. There was a certain amount of curiosity, and not failing for my team was a good motivator, but that was very difficult to do. But after learning it, I'm psyched I know it. And I can have a fruitful conversation with anyone about that stuff, and it feels empowering.

When we were first starting to look at schools for my daughter, there was this phrase that kept coming up called "lifetime learners." This notion of a scholastic environment that promotes the idea of never-ending learning stuck with me. I find it really inspiring.

WHAT THEY SAID, summarized:

- In order to lead, you have to evolve your thinking as the job evolves.
- It's hard to offer value when you're working from memory of how things used to be.
- Leadership is a learned skill that requires continual strengthening.
- You need to address personal weaknesses to grow.
- Curiosity is a good motivator for growth.
- Be a lifetime learner.

Avoid burning a bridge you don't intend to walk across

AVOID BURNING
A BRIDGE YOU
DON'T INTEND
TO WALK ACROSS.

"What's the harm in taking a meeting?" A lot, actually.

Taking a meeting with a potential new company can seem innocuous enough, especially when they say things like, "Hey, no worries, it's just a conversation," and they lavish you with praise and adoration. But tread carefully. When you get an interested suitor's hopes up only to rebuff their advances, they could very well take the rejection personally. Or, if you're using it as a bargaining chip for more money or a loftier position with your current employer, buyer beware. That "no thank you" from you now, after several meetings, might end up being a "no way in hell" from them later.

Right or wrong, the potential inference of being "open to a conversation" is that you're not 100 percent happy where you're working and you're open to a move. By saying no after the conversation, you're implying that, while you're interested in a move, you're not interested in moving to their company. And remember, we're talking about sensitive creative people with fragile egos who don't like to hear the word *no*. Even though you said it in the nicest possible way, it may still sound like a snub to them.

That said, there is some nuance to consider. Talking to other companies is typically the best way to find out if you're getting paid what you're worth and, sadly, the best way to get more from your current employer (there's a tendency for companies to hold off on raises or promotions until someone else is vying for that person). But while it may end up working in your favor short term, with a raise or new title, you are likely permanently shutting a door with the other company. You have to weigh the opportunity costs: Is what you get now worth it versus the opportunity you lose later?

My advice, if you're not serious about the opportunity or not doing it to "seriously" explore your market value, think very carefully about taking the meeting. You can tell them how much you love them and their work, and that they're at the top of your list of places to work in the future, but that you're happy where you are for now. It's much cleaner and avoids the risk of people misconstruing signs, taking rejection too personally, and lighting that bridge on fire.

• •

SAM OLIVER

Group Creative Director, Apple

I THINK IT'S good to talk to other companies if you're honest with your thoughts. If someone calls, and you're not necessarily interested in the place, I'd just be honest and say, "Look, I'm really happy where I am and it doesn't sound quite right for me but I'm happy to have a chat." That way, they go into conversation with you knowing where you stand. And then, if after the chat you still feel the same and they want to further it, then I'd say, "Look, I don't think so." Don't string them along. Be honest about how you're feeling at every juncture, and it's up to them if they want to push it further. Don't string people along and give them hope when there is none.

But on occasion it has worked the other way, where I went into it thinking I'm totally happy and not necessarily ready to make a move, and then I had the chat, and the chat changed my mind. It was really interesting and it actually led to something. So, you never know.

BRIAN MILLER

Creative Director, The Walt Disney Company/ Global Marketing

I'VE HEARD THIS another way from a past, wise creative director boss. He said, "Don't go looking unless you're serious about leaving."

I have "taken the meeting" many times, been flown across the country and put up in a hotel then having staffers take valuable time out of their day to meet with me—all when I knew the moment the plane landed that I was having second thoughts. I feel shitty about that to this day.

• • •

ANGUS WALL

Producer, *13th*; Editor, *The Girl with the Dragon Tattoo*, *The Social Network*;
Founder, Rock Paper Scissors Editorial, A52, Elastic

I THINK THERE'S an art to leaving. To be very truthful without hurting anyone's feelings. To be graceful. To let the people that you're working with know as early on as possible. People who have left a couple jobs already tend to do it better.

WHAT THEY SAID, summarized:

- It's perfectly fine to take meetings, but be honest going into them.
- Don't string a company along.
- When you take a meeting, consider the time and investment being made at your expense.
- Try to avoid hurting feelings when exiting. Share your plans as early as possible.
- Be respectful in the way you leave your current job. Consider the situation your departure might put them in.

THE CAREER

A higher salary only makes
you happy on payday

A HIGHER SALARY ONLY MAKES YOU **YOU HAPPY** ON PAYDAY.

This should be so obvious, yet it isn't: a bigger paycheck isn't going to make you love your job. It's great when you get the raise or offer, and the day you get it can be total euphoria, but happiness ultimately comes from liking what you do, who you do it with, and, when applicable, who you do it for. This is especially true for creative people who, right or wrong, often draw a connection between the things they make and their own self-worth. If you're doing below-average work, the money probably won't be enough to alleviate your daily discontent, frustration, or ego withdrawals. Nor will it be enough to soothe the pangs of regret for leaving your old job to go there.

You need to consider everything when you're looking for a new job, beyond the financial incentives: the work, the people, the clients, the culture. Do your research. If you know someone who works there or who's worked there in the past, get the skinny. Look at their current and past work. Sure, if the current work isn't great, it could be a lack of talent, but chances are it's a lack of vision from the people in the organization. And find out why the role is available. If it's a new role, that's one thing. But if you're replacing someone, it's good to know why. Maybe it was the person. Or maybe it was the place.

And don't go on the promise that if things are bad at the company looking to hire you, they're going to "turn it around." The role of change agent is a difficult one. It takes a lot of time and effort to right a ship, and who knows if it's even feasible? Given the fact that you need to commit to a job based on a few short meetings, you won't really know the full story on a company until you've already started working there. By then it might be too late.

If you're unhappy with the pay at a job you like, then figure out a way to get more. Perhaps there's a way to use a higher-paying job as leverage to negotiate. Or if the money isn't there now, put a plan together with your company to get it there in the future. But don't leave until you've at least given it a go. Money is easier to find than a job that makes you happy.

• •

SUSAN CREDLE

Global Chief Creative Officer, FCB Global

I HAVE A rule. If you don't feel happy for fourteen days doing what you're doing, you should quit. You're not gonna go home happy every day, and you're going to go home miserable some days, but if you can go fourteen days without feeling a sense of happiness, you need to move on.

Knowing who you want to be in the world attracts the right people. I've had a lot of people call and say, "I want to work with you because of what I've heard about you, and what matters to you in the world." And then some people are like, "I don't want to be that. I want to be with the killers. I want a leader that will play the system, be ruthless at all costs, and put winning above everything else." Some people will be attracted to that. It's amazing how I watch certain leaders who will do anything as long as it's legal.

Don't join cultures that aren't reflective of how you're hardwired. A nice, friendly, collaborative culture would cripple some of the people I know.

DAVIS GUGGENHEIM

Producer and Director, *Deadwood, Melrose Place, An Inconvenient Truth, Waiting for Superman, It Might Get Loud*

FOR TEN-PLUS YEARS I was a television director. I would guest direct shows like *NYPD Blue, Alias, ER,* and *24.* It was a very stressful and demanding job, but it paid well. There's a chair that says your name on it and the word DIRECTOR. But when you direct television it's like being a midwife. You're delivering someone else's baby. You didn't conceive it. You're just helping it out into the world. While the fun and glory of directing television was seductive and tantalizing, it lacked the meaning and purpose of having something you yourself have created. So I made the scary decision to leave that world and start making my own documentaries. That choice had huge ramifications on my life. It was a huge pay cut, by a very large factor, and there was tremendous uncertainty. If you don't have a film you're making, you don't have a job. Once your film is finished, you're not sure if and when you'll have another. The budgets are much lower. And in a documentary, there is no prestige of sitting in a chair with your name on it—instead, you spend a lot of your time in the back of a rented minivan eating cold sandwiches.

I needed to find work that had more meaning and where I had more creative control. And I found that in documentaries.

JONATHAN CAVENDISH

Producer, *Bridget Jones's Diary, Elizabeth: The Golden Age, Mowgli: Legend of the Jungle*; Founder, The Imaginarium Studios

I WOULDN'T HAVE done what I've done if my overriding interest was money. If that was the case, I would have stayed in advertising and made a ton of money.

TARAS WAYNER

Chief Creative Officer, Saatchi & Saatchi

I HAVE MADE it a rule to *never* take a job or even hire someone without explaining my vision for what I believe makes great work and how I want to get there. And to ask my new boss or employee what their vision is. If everything aligns, then we both know we're connected over a vision, and we can immediately start making plans to get to great work together. If we don't agree, which is perfectly fine, I know that we shouldn't be working together.

WHAT THEY SAID, summarized:

- Make sure you're going home happy most days.
- Determine the type of culture that appeals to you.
- Make sure your job is keeping you fulfilled.
- Sometimes happiness means taking a risk and leaving some comforts behind.
- It's important to be sure your vision aligns with the company's vision.

go away
and stay away

GO AWAY
AND STAY AWAY.

Too many of us are guilty of staying tethered to work at all times. We spend our hard earned vacations staring into our laptops by resort pools, pacing hotel lobbies on conference calls, and looking for Wi-Fi connections at every venue or event so we can check our email. Rather than spending our time off decompressing with our loved ones, we're busy quarterbacking projects back at the office. And who of us isn't guilty of texting-while-parenting? All of us who have seen the "shame scowl" at an elementary school performance say "aye." Aye!

Whenever we attempt to get away, we bring our pocket-sized suitcases, filled with all the stress of our jobs. We've become work prisoners in an always-on culture. However, there are benefits to completely unplugging and ditching our devices. For one, it's a legit chance to recharge. When you can get all those micro- and macro-stressors off your plate and out of your brain, even if it's just for a square or two on your kitten-themed wall calendar, it can get you back to peak mental condition and help to avoid burnout. And when you return to work, you come back 100 percent energized and ready to dive back in, as opposed to slightly worn down.

When you fully disconnect, you don't risk having your time away ruined by bad news. Any worst-case scenarios playing out back at home will be dark clouds looming over you that won't allow any sunshine through the cracks. And even though there's nothing you can do to change things, it's now a permanent damper on the moment.

Another positive aspect of disconnecting is that it empowers people on your team to be the decisionmakers. They're forced into leadership positions, which gives them the training and experience they need if they're going to get to the next level. That, in turn, is going to make them more confident and secure in their roles, which is going to make it easier for you to walk away and fully disconnect without being concerned the whole time.

Lastly, disconnecting is a way of setting boundaries with your workplace. If you're a talented creative person or leader, or your company has too much work for too few people, they're going to pile on as much work as they can. In all likelihood, they won't stop adding to your workload until you tell them to stop. And, if you're a people pleaser or anxious about your job, no is a hard thing to tell folks. However, it's important to establish parameters with your company. There's nothing wrong with asking them to respect your personal time and a work-life balance. (It runs both ways, too—respecting your out of office on vacation tells your employees that they're not expected to be on call 24/7, either.)

Now go get your bathing suit on. And please, do us all a favor and leave your phone in the room.

• •

SCOTT TRATTNER

Former VP, Executive Creative Director, Facebook; former Executive Director, TBWA\Media Arts Lab

HOW CAN YOU create balance in a world that demands focus on the big rock you're pushing up the hill, where creativity isn't something that can necessarily be cracked between the hours of nine and five?

It's important to your creativity and career longevity to disconnect, but the devil is in the details. Creating balance for yourself is a complicated thing. On one side, it's critical to any endeavor, whether you're creative or not, that you have this outlet and life outside work that fuels you. On the other side, with the demands of any business today, you need to be all over it 24/7.

I think the place where we need to be selfish is self-care, in all its machinations, from creativity to exercise to family bonding. It will help you perform better, longer. But I think the trick is how to finesse that into your working life. If you're at a place where you're not getting that opportunity, you need to get it. Now, you might be in a period in your career where you're doubling or tripling down on what you're doing. While you feel good sustaining that pace, do it. But at some point you may not feel as good doing it, and that's when you should stop. When you're not feeling inspired, challenged, or like you're not having impact, you've gotta change. It's like that old Steve Jobs quote: "If today were the last day of my life, would I want to do what I am about to do today?"

EMILY MCDOWELL

Founder, Creative Director, Emily McDowell & Friends; Author, *There Is No Good Card for This*

I STARTED TO set limits for myself. I was getting so burned out. When I'd get notes in the mail from people that say things like, "This thing you wrote repaired my relationship with my dad," and I couldn't even get satisfaction from it, I knew something was wrong. I was so exhausted that I didn't care about anything besides getting work done.

DAVID OYELOWO

Actor, *Selma*; Producer, *Come Away*; Director, *The Water Man*

THE LEVEL OF your performance and quality of your output is tied to the time you take away.

As an actor and director, my job is to reflect humanity back to humanity. And you can only do that if you are engaging in humanity in a very real way that is devoid of the Hollywood artifice. It's superficial. And if you've had any modicum of success, you're surrounded by "yes people." In what I do, success is incredibly erosive to the ability to tell the truth. So it's a very active and intentional thing to take time away from all the BS and go engage with humanity.

There's a reason why the most potent performances or work you see from people come in their first few performances. They either start to work too much or they start to disengage with the reality that was infusing their first performances. And its only when they find ways to walk away from Hollywood that they get their mojo back. It's important to actively take time away, maintain reality checks in your life (like family), have hobbies, or work with causes that are antithetical to the nonsense of the production world.

In my industry, there's something very counterintuitive to taking breaks because it is such a competitive industry and, as the adage goes, "you're only as good as your last project." If it wasn't a success, which more often than not they're not as successful as you'd like, there's a feeling like "I should get back in the saddle." But taking time off is essential to keeping your connection to humanity intact and your creative tank full.

• • •

WHAT THEY SAID, summarized:

- It's important to your creativity and career longevity to disconnect.
- Set limits for yourself.
- Try to carve out balance.
- Find outlets for yourself.
- Be selfish about self-care.
- Your investment in your work is also determined by where you are in your career.

We all need a "fuck it" bucket

WE ALL NEED A "FUCK IT" BUCKET.

Most creative people experience some degree of self-doubt and anxiety. We feel like imposters just waiting to be discovered for who we really are. We think that the last great thing that we created might very well be the last great thing we ever create. We blame ourselves a little too harshly when things go wrong. And it only gets worse when our role in making things is limited to oversight. Fear, insecurity, and self-doubt can be crippling, both physically and mentally, and they can manifest themselves in the unhealthy ways we deal with teams that work for and with us. Add to that a high-stress job where we're constantly expected to generate great ideas, scripts, designs, edits, stories, and products faster and better than anyone else out there, and it's a breakdown or career change waiting to happen.

Which is why we all need ourselves a "fuck it" bucket, a theoretical place we can deposit those needless worries and concerns that continually plague us. The fuck it bucket, which one website referred to as "the bastard child of *Shit Happens* and *Don't Worry, Be Happy*," is a way to cope with the undue stress, anxiety, self-doubt, and failures that come with our high-pressure creative jobs. Sure, it's an extremely narrow and trivial solution to a complicated problem, but it serves to illustrate a point: when we're faced with moments of self-doubt or personal failure, we need a way to reduce the internalization of stress and anxiety. A healthier perspective of what's truly important in life can remedy some of that personal distress and help us get through tougher times. Work didn't sell. Fuck it, you're not perfect and you'll get the next one. Talented creative person quits. Fuck it, another great one will come along. Angry client. Fuck it, you did your best and hopefully it works out. Boss threatens your job. Fuck it, if this one doesn't work out you'll get a new one. Go on, fill that fuck it bucket up.

Beyond filling up your fuck it bucket, there are other, more practical ways of getting your head into a good, fuck it–worthy place. Things like yoga, meditation, sports, meaningful chats with friends, or a hundred thousand other activities can help reduce the debilitating symptoms of self-doubt and anxiety. At the end of the day, we all deserve happy, healthy careers, doing work we enjoy with people we (mostly) like. And if that means changing jobs or talking with a therapist on a regular basis, to paraphrase Nike: *just fucking do it.*

• •

MIKE ALDERSON

Cofounder and Chief Creative Officer, Man vs. Machine

I'D JUST TURNED thirty. It had been five years of running my own production company with my partner. We didn't have a producer. We did everything ourselves because, well, we didn't think anyone could do it as well as us. I was continually adding responsibilities to my list and never delegating or taking things off my plate. I had an obsessive need for everything to be perfect, and failure was never an option.

My sickness began as a lingering dizziness, something like a "mind fog," where I was having trouble being able to stay focused and maintain my energy. I tried my best to ignore it and didn't tell anyone, not even my wife. This went on for about a year, but it continued to worsen, to the point that it became a

constant and debilitating exhaustion. Perhaps the best way to explain it is "tiredness, but amplified by one thousand." I could no longer pretend I wasn't suffering and went to see my physician.

I didn't think I was stressed, because my company was doing great and having lots of success. Also, at that age, you think you're indestructible. But I was feeling so badly that I needed to get checked out by a doctor. I went through the long process of crossing physical ailments off the list. They started with the ears, then the eyes, then moved on to the brain. I got a test for everything. It was really scary. Finally, after a battery of tests for multiple sclerosis came up negative, the neurologist said, "We could keep doing tests, but I have a feeling this is a stress-related disorder." Even though many people, including my wife, had already reached this conclusion, being a simple, proud bloke from Northern England, I just couldn't accept it. Now I was finally ready.

The next day, I spoke to my business partner and said I needed to take some time off. I said I needed to reduce my mental stress and anxiety. He understood.

I knew I'd made the huge mistake of ignoring it, and realized that since it was such a long journey in, there was absolutely no way it was going to be a short journey out. I didn't go into the office. I tried taking walks, but I was so broken I couldn't even gather the energy to do that. I meditated, even though the feeling of switching off my brain was so foreign to me. Someone suggested reflexology, so I did that, too. And I rested, but of course your brain is always trying to trick you and wants to use the time away to do something else. You have to be able to say, "No, that's not the idea," and shut things down. The big objectives were to teach myself to relax and manage my personal expectations—which took a lot of time and wasn't easy to accept. In Britain, mental health is not in the best place. You don't talk about it, and it's all about having a stiff upper lip and "just getting through it." Yet, surprisingly, once the word got out through East London about my condition, I actually had several industry peers contact me privately and say, "I've gone through what you're going through. You'll be back."

I ended up returning after six months. Hard as it was, I had to lower my expectations for myself. I stopped involving myself in every single micro-problem or detail. I picked the battles worth fighting, and, knowing that as soon as I walked into a room I was going to immerse myself in whatever was going on, I chose the rooms I entered carefully.

I wanted to make sure I didn't return to the old, full-tilt Mike and have a relapse. Since my London apartment was synonymous with stress and anxiety, my wife and I got a house in the countryside by the sea, where I could establish a new set of behaviors each weekend. The phone would go in a wooden box outside of the house. There was a big garden and beach for me to use to get into the right headspace.

I think stress and anxiety are in all of us, but depending on the individual, it can live closer or further from the surface. After fourteen years of doing this job, I'm now fully aware of the best way to deal with my stress and anxiety. Yes, I still struggle to implement it every single day, but I am changing. I have to.

SUSAN CREDLE

Global Chief Creative Officer, FCB Global

SHOW UP AS positively as you can. Show up as present as you can. Do the best you can. And, by the way, when you're bummed out or pissed off, have a pissed-off, bummed-out day. But then get over it and get back out there.

It's an emotional job. It's a subjective job. It's a struggle every day. There are a lot of feelings on the line, more than I've seen in a lot of businesses. I think it's important to maintain a perspective. And I think you should try to stay true to your values and be a good person whenever possible. You might not operate there all the time, but know when you've gone wrong and know how to correct. You may not be perfect every day, but you can try really, really hard.

SCOTT MARDER

Executive Producer, *Rick and Morty, The Mick, It's Always Sunny in Philadelphia*

I FANTASIZE ABOUT simple jobs. A guy who works construction, he hammers some wood, the day ends, and he leaves. There's nothing he can do until he goes back tomorrow. Sounds pretty good sometimes.

LANCE JENSEN

Chief Creative Officer, Hill Holliday

SOME DAYS I think, "You did pretty good today," and other days I think, "You have no right to be doing this." Either way, I go back and do it all again the next day. You have to.

WHAT THEY SAID, summarized:

- It's important to manage your stress and anxiety.
- Try to maintain perspective and show up as positively as you can each day.
- Push through the bad days and self-doubt.

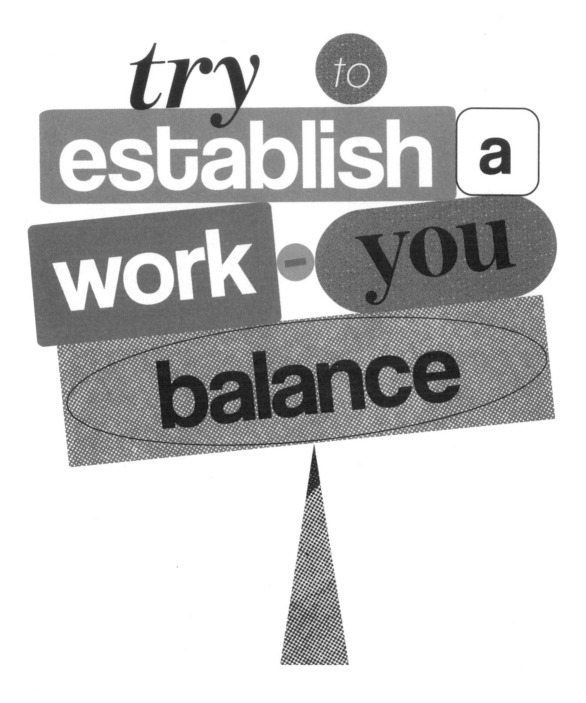

TRY TO ESTABLISH
A WORK-YOU
BALANCE.

n Europe, this isn't advice—it's common sense. Many of us pour a ton of energy and passion into our craft, in many cases on behalf of other people and companies. Too often it's at the expense of our personal health and happiness. We'll work day and night perfecting our presentations, sharpening our scripts, assembling our edits, rendering our sketches, and churning out idea after idea after idea, and what gets lost is what's truly important in our lives: our families, our outside interests, and our self-care.

It's important to remember that, as you give so much of yourself to your jobs and your work, you don't forget about *you*. Try to do something for yourself every day if you can, whether it's some form of personal enrichment, physical activity, or spending meaningful time with people you love. You'll feel better about yourself. And, ultimately, a better you makes better work.

I've created a space in my house where I can play records and read graphic novels and my wife can do her *New York Times* crossword puzzle (I realize how disgustingly domestic that sounds, and so I apologize), and shake free the stresses of our days.

Here's what some people do to establish their work-you balance:

• • •

ANGUS WALL

Producer, *13th*; Editor, *The Girl with the Dragon Tattoo*,
The Social Network; Founder, Rock Paper Scissors
Editorial, A52, Elastic

BEING A PHYSICAL athlete helps me be a better business athlete. You feel good psychologically when you feel good physically. Running is active meditation. I run six days a week and crash out on the seventh day. I read a lot, too. Ironically, I don't watch much content at all.

SCOTT TRATTNER

Former VP, Executive Creative Director, Facebook;
former Executive Director, TBWA\Media Arts Lab

THE DIRECTOR FREDERICK Bond is a good friend of mine. He challenged me to come to his house and try an ice bath. I thought, sure, this will be a novelty. And I loved it. It's beautiful. It's so pure. The best thing about taking ice baths is, when you immerse yourself in such cold water, the only thing that matters is finding your breath. You can't worry about the stress you're carrying around, a meeting, a looming deadline, my wife who's angry at me—none of that matters because all you're trying to do is find your breath.

• • •

SCOTT MARDER

Executive Producer, *Rick and Morty*,
The Mick, It's Always Sunny in Philadelphia

I GET MADE fun of for this, but sometimes after a long workday I'll go to the supermarket, even though we don't need anything, and I'll just walk the aisles. There's something very meditative and peaceful about it.

RACHEL SHUKERT

Co-Executive Producer, *GLOW*;
Executive Producer, *The Baby-Sitters Club*

WE'RE ALL SO plugged in, and making a show is so much work. But now that I have a family and a toddler, it mandates turn-off time. The first few hours of each day and the last hour before bedtime, it's just about us.

I do believe in burnout. Not necessarily with ideas, but with the will to execute them. Desire is a less renewable resource than creativity. I have to conserve it. I only have so many hours where I can be creative. I am very "in it" when I'm in it, but when I'm done, there's no reason to force it. I try to pay attention to my natural rhythm.

SHANNON WASHINGTON

Group Executive Creative Director, R/GA

I WILL ANGRY cook. That's where, as you're making stuff, you're like, "Fuck this," and, "Fuck that." I might not even be that hungry, but I'm getting everything in me out and releasing my energy so that by the end I'm feeling like me again.

MATT DRENIK

Creative Director, SOUTH Music and Sound Design; Recording Artist, El Camino Media, Sony Music Entertainment

MY WAY TO get my mind off of music is to take walks and think about other creative projects. Walks help me build bridges to other creative ideas.

RON RADZINER

President, Design Partner, Marmol Radziner Architects

I WAKE UP at four thirty and I'm in the office by five thirty every morning. I have some tea and am able to spend the next couple of hours drawing. When most people begin to come in, the rest of the day is usually meetings with staff and clients.

SUSAN CREDLE

Global Chief Creative Officer, FCB Global

DECOMPRESSION, FOR ME, is realizing that there's a bigger world out there than this and thinking about how, in the grand scheme of things, very little of this will matter. It's shifting my perspective to thinking about how big this universe is and how small my place in it is.

SUSAN HOFFMAN

Chairman, Wieden & Kennedy

GET SATISFACTION FROM your job. Love your job. Part of my good fortune is that I've worked in different offices. If I'd been only in our Portland, Oregon, office my whole career, I would not have grown. That has been invaluable training to learn different cultures and different styles of management. So, instead of working for different companies, I gained a similar experience with our different offices. I opened up Amsterdam and London and oversaw New York and have spent time in all the offices.

I'm a bit of a workaholic, and that's not always good. But I grew up in a time when women weren't expected to be successful, so that plays into this. My kids are certainly a good diversion for me. Should I find more important things outside of Wieden? Yeah, probably. But it's been such a fun rollercoaster ride.

JON IKEDA

VP, Acura Brand Officer
and former Lead Designer, Acura

I'M AN INTROVERT by nature, even though I'm thrown in front of people all the time. And now there's no turning off. Any time I can be alone is a luxury. I like being alone on a plane or in the airport. I put the headphones on and I get hours to be alone. Just me.

SURESH NAIR

Global Chief Strategy Officer, Grey Worldwide

I'VE CANCELED MORE vacations than I care to remember and I work a lot of weekends, but I try to make up for them. We have gone on lots of family trips but—sigh—I've always got my iPad or laptop. Yes, it's a long leash, but it does allow us to go away.

MARCELLA COAD

Creative Director, Amazon

I'M REALLY GOOD at turning off when I leave for the day. In fact, I get mad when people want to talk about work after work. It's why I don't like working from home. I like that feeling of separation.

AVA DUVERNAY

Executive Producer, *Queen Sugar*;
Director, *When They See Us*, *Selma*, *A Wrinkle in Time*

I DON'T GIVE back to myself. I'm really bad at that. It took me a while to realize that I'm really happiest when I'm working. Maybe it comes from picking up a camera at thirty-two years old, maybe it comes from looking at my industry and seeing there aren't many black women doing it, or feeling like I have to fit everything in a certain window of time. But I enjoy my days. I don't want to be sitting on a beach, or playing racquetball, or whatever the hell people do for self-care. I want to be talking to people, learning, making things, writing, reading scripts, on set. Those things are a joy and privilege and that so many people don't get to enjoy. It's not a burden at all.

EMILY MCDOWELL

Founder, Creative Director, Emily McDowell & Friends;
Author, *There Is No Good Card for This*

I MEDITATE, DO breath work, yoga, and have recently gotten back into spirituality.

GUTO TERNI

Partner, Director, ROOF Animation Studio

TWO YEARS AGO, I established an exercise for myself. When I get home, I study guitar for ninety minutes a day. This is my meditation. It empties your head and allows you to focus on one thing.

VALERIE VAN GALDER

CEO, Depressed Cake Shop; Producer,
former President of Marketing, Sony Pictures

I QUIT. That's why I'm no longer on the "The Powerful Women in Hollywood" list anymore.

LANCE JENSEN

Chief Creative Officer, Hill Holliday

I'M NOT VERY good at living. But I'm working on it.

WHEN I FIRST TOOK A LEADERSHIP POSITION,
I WISH I WOULD HAVE . . .

XANTHE WELLS

Senior Director, Global Executive Creative Director,
Devices & Services, Google

. . . not based my leadership style off of men who were not at all like me. There was one man who I modeled myself after who was loud, super masculine, and physically imposing, all the things that I'm not. I was trying to do something that wasn't true to me. I wish at the time I had more confidence in my leadership style, which is more of a bottoms-up, of-the-people approach.

MIKE ALDERSON

Cofounder and Chief Creative Officer, Man vs. Machine

. . . known what I was getting into. I wasn't prepared for what was coming. It was literally two graphic designers in a room, starting a company, at twenty-five years old, so I didn't know what to expect.

SURESH NAIR

Global Chief Strategy Officer, Grey Worldwide

. . . had more trust in my abilities. When I was promoted I thought, "Can I even do this?" Suddenly I had many more people working for me, some more senior than me. I thought, "Are they going to trust my instinct and direction? Are they going to buy what I'm saying? Or will they think I'm just some young Turk?"

MARCELLA COAD

Creative Director, Amazon

. . . **NOT. I FEEL LIKE** mentoring and working with junior creative people is more fulfilling than managing. But, fortunately, Amazon allows me to sidestep the typical management role and be a more senior-level creative person.

AVA DUVERNAY

Executive Producer, *Queen Sugar*; Director,
When They See Us, Selma, A Wrinkle in Time

. . . **TRUSTED PEOPLE MORE.** I kept a lot close to the vest because I only trusted myself. I should have let go a little earlier than I did. It would have helped me a lot, and it would have empowered people sooner. I eventually got to a place where I trust people . . . until you prove I can't.

DUNCAN MILNER

Former Global Creative President,
Media Arts Lab, MAL For Good

. . . **NOT BELIEVED SO MUCH** in my own ideas. That transition from coming up with ideas to inspiring someone else to come up with ideas is a tough one. When you come up as a creative person, you have to believe in your ideas more than anyone else. But all of a sudden you have to be open to someone else's ideas first and stop yourself from developing their work.

EMILY MCDOWELL

Founder, Creative Director, Emily McDowell & Friends;
Author, *There Is No Good Card for This*

. . . **KNOWN WHAT KIND OF** boundaries to set with my employees, from the kind of language I used with them, to the frequency of emails I'd send at all hours. I wish I could have regulated those things, been more of a calming presence with them, and not let my stress impact those relationships.

JEFF GILES

Executive Editor, *Vanity Fair*;
Author, *The Edge of Everything*

. . . **BEEN MORE EMPATHETIC** and more humane. There were definitely some people who I edited in the very beginning who I've never heard from again. I've learned that the human part of the job is so important.

RAVI NAIDOO

Founder, Design Indaba; CEO, Interactive Africa

. . . **HAD MORE CREATIVE COURAGE.** Coming from life sciences, I suffered from imposter syndrome. Even though I had a native intelligence, I felt like an imposter because I didn't specialize in that particular area.

INDEX

ABOUT THE AUTHOR

JASON SPERLING currently serves as global executive creative director for Facebook Reality Labs. He has worked in advertising and marketing for more than two decades, developing iconic work for clients that include Apple, Honda, TikTok, Disney, Amazon, UNICEF Worldwide, and many others.

Among his notable achievements, Jason was selected in 2015 by *Adweek* as one of the Top 30 Creative Directors in the country. His work for Honda has won numerous top international awards, as well as an Emmy nomination. His *"Mac vs. PC"* campaign was declared Campaign of the Decade by *Adweek* and listed among the Top 10 Campaigns of the Century by *AdAge.* And his *Imaginary Friend Society* film series, which explains the many facets of the pediatric cancer experience, has been translated into more than a dozen languages and is being used by hospitals worldwide.

His first book, *Look at Me When I'm Talking to You: Building Brand Attraction in an Age of Brand Aversion*, was released on Instagram (@lookatmebook). It was launched a page a day for more than 160 days in order to demonstrate the need to break through in today's challenging media environment.

Jason lives in Los Angeles. He is married to Nicole and is dad to Hannah, Natalie, and Will.

ABOUT THE ILLUSTRATOR

LAUNDRY is a leading branding, design, animation, and VFX studio with offices in Los Angeles and San Francisco.

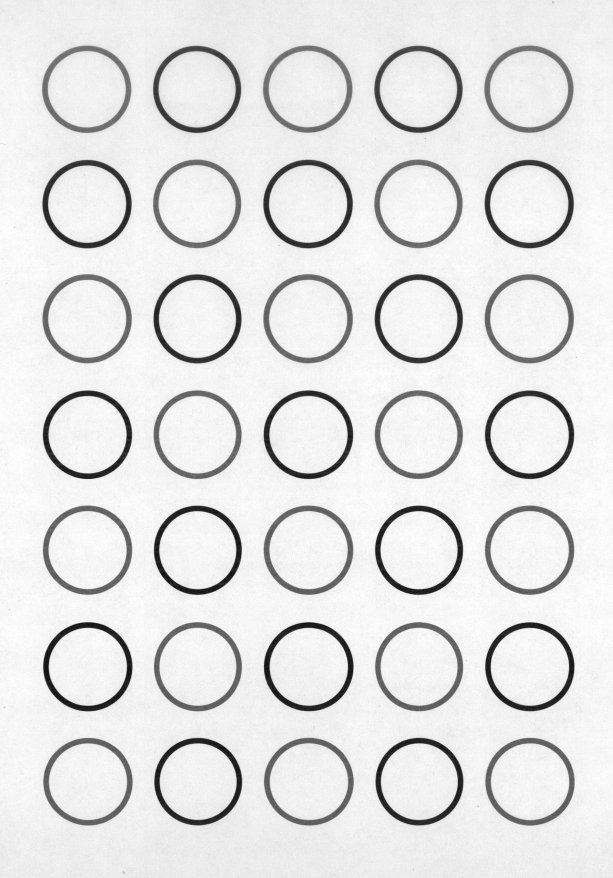